ST. ANTONY'S PAPERS · NUMBER 22

★

LATIN AMERICAN AFFAIRS

ST. ANTONY'S PAPERS

published by Messrs. Chatto and Windus Ltd.

★

published by Oxford University Press

ST. ANTONY'S PAPERS · NUMBER 22

LATIN AMERICAN AFFAIRS

EDITED BY

RAYMOND CARR

OXFORD UNIVERSITY PRESS

1970

Oxford University Press, Ely House, London W. 1

GLASGOW NEW YORK TORONTO MELBOURNE WELLINGTON
CAPE TOWN SALISBURY IBADAN NAIROBI DAR ES SALAAM LUSAKA ADDIS ABABA
BOMBAY CALCUTTA MADRAS KARACHI LAHORE DACCA
KUALA LUMPUR SINGAPORE HONG KONG TOKYO

PRINTED IN GREAT BRITAIN
BY BILLING & SONS LIMITED
GUILDFORD AND LONDON

To

F. W. DEAKIN

whose energy and vision
created the College
of which he was Warden 1950–68

CONTENTS

The main emphasis of the work of St. Antony's College, Oxford, since its foundation in 1950 has been in the fields of modern history and international affairs. The College organizes a number of regular Seminars at which are read papers produced by its members in the course of their research or by visiting experts from other institutions. The College further sponsors the delivery of lectures in Oxford by scholars of international reputation in their respective fields.

An appreciable volume of contribution to scholarship is thus being produced under the auspices of St. Antony's and the present series was started in order to preserve and present a selection of this work. The series is not, however, confined to this material alone and may include contributions from other places.

Each number is devoted to a particular topic or a particular part of the world.

The studies on which the essays in this volume are based were aided by a generous grant from the Ford Foundation.

SOCIETY AND MASS REBELLION IN EIGHTEENTH-CENTURY PERU AND BOLIVIA*

by Oscar Cornblit

I

IN 1780, an impressive series of mass rebellions broke out in a region which covered the southern parts of present Peru and the western and northern areas of Bolivia. This series of outbreaks has since been labelled as the Tupac Amarú rebellion. Geographically, the rebellions spread from Cuzco, in Peru, down to Jujuy, in Argentina; but the chief and more violent centres remained within the area bounded by the cities of Cuzco and Potosí. The revolts continued for two years, reaching their climax in 1781.

Casualties are difficult to estimate. There is some sparse evidence as to their extent, from anti-rebel sources: deaths probably reached several tens of thousands on the loyalist side[1]—in the siege of La Paz alone, there is an estimate of 6,000 deaths. Losses on the 'Indian' side are even more difficult to calculate. Without doubt they were higher than those of the loyalist, as eyewitness accounts confirm. Deaths were very high for such a small population, perhaps 100,000 out of 2,000,000.[2] The economic repercussions of these rebellions

---

* This paper was written during the author's sojourn as Visiting Fellow at St. Antony's College, Oxford, on the basis of a paper presented to the Latin American Seminars in Hilary Term 1968. His particular indebtedness goes to Professor Raymond Carr, Mr. Alan Angell, Mr. Malcolm Deas, and Mr. Ezequiel Gallo.

[1] In his diary of the siege, Sebastian de Segurola says that a third of the population of the city of La Paz were killed during the siege: 'Diario de los Sucesos del Cerro de la Ciudad de La Paz', in Vicente de Ballivian y Roxas, *Archivo Boliviano. Colección de documentos relativos a la historia de Bolivia en la época colonial*, Tomo I (Paris: A. Franck, 1872), p. 63. The population of La Paz was about 20,000 persons at that time. See *La Paz en su IV Centenario 1548–1948*, Vol. I (Edición del Comité pro IV Centenario de la Fundación de La Paz, Bs. Aires, 1948), p. 31.

[2] Hernandez Sanchez–Barba estimates that the population of present Bolivia and Peru was about 2,200,000 by the end of the eighteenth century: *La Sociedad Colonial Americana en el siglo XVIII* in J. Vicens Vives, *Historia de España y América*, IV (Editorial Vicens Vives, Barcelona, 1961), p. 339. A contemporary writer

were disastrous. In addition to the destruction of capital goods, the government expenditure on defence costs rose to about 2,650,000 pesos. This sum was equivalent to the annual revenue of the Peruvian viceroyalty.[3]

Even this figure does not represent total expenditure. The rebels forced their opponents to mobilize all available local resources; the whole of the population in the region was affected by, and involved in, the struggles. Consequently, the contribution of the private sector was also very important both in terms of money and in human resources.

These data indicate the exceptional nature of the revolts in 1780 and must therefore be carefully assessed. Riots, disturbances, 'turmoils', the killing of government officials such as *corregidores*, were not uncommon in Peruvian colonial life during the eighteenth century. Throughout the century, riots had taken place. For example, before the great revolt of 1780, there was the 1730 rising in Cochabamba; there are reports of outbreaks in 1739 in Oruro (Velar de Córdoba), of fighting in 1742 in Tarma and Jauja (Juan Santos Atahualpa) which continued to 1750, and of the 1750 rising in Huarochiri by a group who killed the corregidor Villa de Moros. The rioters 'set fire to his house, killed him and the rest of the people in his company, savagely mutilating their corpses; they ate their tongues and used their skulls as drinking vessels. When this was done, without further ceremony they threw the former corregidor and a servant over a cliff. After this, they devoted themselves to recruiting troops, breaking up roads, destroying bridges, and spreading insurrection to the neighbouring villages.'[4]

The authorities did not always resort to vigorous repression. When, in 1776 Corregidor Jerónimo Sagasti of the province of Chumbivilcas met the same fate as Villa de Moros, Viceroy Guirior retaliated by lowering taxes and filing away the case as inconspicuously

estimates a total of 100,000 Indian deaths of all kinds. See Rafael José Sahuaraura Titu Atauchi, *Estado del Perú* (1784) (Francisco A. Loayza, Lima, 1944), p. 14. David Forbes gives a total of 40,000 deaths for the Spaniards: *The Aymará Indians* (London: Taylor and Francis, 1870), p. 6.

[3] For these data, see Guillermo Cespedes del Castillo, 'Lima y Buenos Aires. Repercusiones económicas y políticas de la creación del Virreynato del Río de la Plata', *Anuario de Estudios Americanos*, III (1946), pp. 743–4, 818. He estimates a total revenue for the four-year period between 1773 and 1776 at 10,186,712 pesos (of 8 reals); but this was perhaps a little less than what was collected.

[4] Manuel de Mendiburu, *Diccionario Histórico-Biográfico del Perú* (2nd ed., Lima, 1933), VII, p. 201.

as possible.[5] Thus, prior to 1780 the authorities were quite familiar with localized riots and disturbances. When one examines the voluminous information which was being channelled to the higher authorities of these regions, to the *Audiencias* (higher courts of justice), to the viceroyalties of Lima and Buenos Aires, and to the Council of the Indies in Spain, on the subject of menaces, physical violence, rumours of upheavals, the impression gathered is that the authorities were already overburdened with these rebellions. They perhaps accepted them as a permanent feature of colonial society in those areas.[6] What, then, are the peculiar characteristics of the 1780 rebellions, which give them their wide and unparalleled extension? May both the geographical extent and limits of these rebellions give us a clue to the dynamic forces operating underneath?

One of these rebellions was that of Juan Santos Atahualpa. It lasted for a period of more than thirteen years, far longer than that of 1780; its leadership seems to have been of the same kind as that of Tupac Amarú. Juan Santos Atahualpa was a formidable leader in that he was provided with intelligence, knowledge, and charisma.[7] Yet his rebellion failed to transform itself into a widespread insurrection, and remained bounded within the Tarma and Jauja frontier regions.

Thus, before dealing with the success of the 1780 rebellion, I shall briefly describe its characteristics in the context of the society within which it broke out.

II

One of the outbreaks of 1780, under the direct leadership of José Gabriel Tupac-Amarú (whose surname was really Condorcanqui),[8] started on 4 November of that year in the province of Tinta.

[5] Mendiburu, op. cit., II, p. 46.

[6] See for instance Archivo General de Indias (*A.G.I*), Audiencia de Charcas, Legajos 591–4, for a small sample of the kind of information which was continuously converging on the Crown officials, from every point of the vast empire.

[7] Juan Santos Atahualpa described himself as an Inca of Cuzco and a supporter of the Christian faith. He could speak Latin, Spanish, and Quechua, and had been taught by Jesuit priests. See letter to Father Fray José Gil Muñoz from Fray Manuel del Santo, Fray José Cabanes, and Fray Domingo García, dated 1742, in Francisco A. Loayza, *Juan Santos el Invencible* (Manuscritos del año de 1742 al año de 1755, Lima, 1942), pp. 1–8.

[8] It might be suggestive to point out that José Gabriel Condorcanqui was not of pure Indian blood. He claimed descent from Felipe Tupac Amarú, leader of a revolt against the Viceroy Francisco de Toledo in the year 1572. Felipe Tupac Amarú was considered a descendant of one of the Inca Rulers, Huayna Capac.

In 1780 there were also many disturbances in other areas: in Arequipa, rebellions broke out on 1 January 1780; on 13 April a conspiracy involving Lorenzo Farfan de los Godos and others was discovered and rapidly suppressed in Cuzco, and several of its leaders condemned to death; other places also witnessed insurrection attempts, such as Moquegua (near Arequipa), Huancavelica, Huaraz, Pasco, and La Plata.[9]

There are discrepancies in the interpretations of the nature of these rebellions. Some authors believed that they involved a different network of interests than that of Tupac Amarú. However, when analysing the so-called Chayanta or Catari uprising, historians point to similarities with the 4 November insurrection. The Catari rebellion, which developed in the province of Chayanta in the audiencia of Charcas (Bolivia), an area between present-day cities of Oruro and Sucre, was already well under way by July and August of 1780. Afterwards the disturbances appeared to settle down, but the murder of its leader, Tomas Catari, triggered off a new wave of violence which culminated in the siege of the city of La Plata (Chuquisaca) in February 1781. By March 1781, rebellion was widespread throughout the area between Cuzco and Potosí. It even extended further south reaching the province of Tucumán in the viceroyalty of Río de la Plata, although there it did not have the character of a mass movement it had attained in the original area.

The main foci of insurrection at the beginning of 1781 were as follows:

1. The Cuzco region, covering the zone between the city of Cuzco and the shores of Lake Titicaca. Leadership here was provided by José Gabriel Tupac Amarú from 4 November 1780, until his defeat on 5 April 1781. He was captured the following day and after trial put to a barbarous death on 18 May.

2. The Puno region, including parts of the *corregimientos* of Lampa and Chucuito on the west, south-west, and south borders of the Lake Titicaca. The region was increasingly devastated by rebellious

---

If the genealogy of José Gabriel Condorcanqui is acceptable, a marriage took place between a grandson of Felipe Tupac Amarú and a Spanish woman called Francisca de Torres. For José Gabriel Tupac Amarú's genealogical claims, see Francisco Loayza (ed.) *Genealogía de Tupac Amarú* (Lima, 1946), pp. 4–58, manuscript taken from *A.G.I.*, Audiencia de Lima, Legajo 1619.

[9] In Boleslao Lewin, *La Rebelión de Tupac Amarú* (Buenos Aires, Hachette, 1957), pp. 184 ff., brief references to these uprisings are made.

bands, which by the middle of January 1781, were practically in control of the whole countryside. Local leadership emerged here from improvised chieftains. Later, they received some support from Diego Tupac Amarú, brother of José Gabriel. Fighting continued from February to May 1781, with the rebel forces attacking the city of Puno. Pressure on Puno was finally so great that the two Royalist chiefs, Orellana and Del Valle, decided to abandon it on 26 May, and retreat to Cuzco.[10]

3. Another focus of revolt was Oruro. Tension increased gradually during December 1780, inside the city until it exploded on January into a bloody unheaval under the leadership of the wealthy Rodriguez brothers, one of whom was proprietor of a silver mine near Oruro. Both brothers were born in Oruro and were of Spanish descent.[11]

This revolt was successful, gaining control of the city. Although around March conflicts emerged within the ranks of the rebels, the Rodriguez brothers were able to keep the situation within controllable limits. During the first period of the Oruro revolt, participation of Indian and half-castes was very high, and the city was continuously invaded by huge crowds which pressed strongly for their demands. Popular pressure was so powerful that the authorities, headed by Jacinto Rodriguez, even decided to dress in typical Indian style.[12]

4. The region surrounding La Paz, and extending towards the south and east of the Lake Titicaca, might be described as another centre of rebellion. There, the most important leader was Julian Apaza, an Indian of Aymará origin. He took the name of Tupac Catari, and directed the siege of the city of La Paz, the most important military event in the history of the rebellions. The siege started in the middle of March 1781, and continued until October of the

[10] 'Relación del cacique de Puno, de sus expediciones, sitios, defensa y varios acontecimientos, hasta que despobló la villa de orden del Sr. Inspector y Comandante General D. José Antonio del Valle. Corre desde 16 de noviembre de 1780 hasta 17 de julio de 1781', p. 100, in Vol. V of De Angelis, Colección de Obras y Documentos Relativos a la Historia Antigua y Moderna de las Provincias del Río de la Plata (Buenos Aires: Imprenta del Estado, 1st ed.) 1836.

[11] See 'Relación de los hechos más notables acaecidos en la sublevación general fraguada . . .' Revista de Archivos y Bibliotecas Nacionales (Lima), III, vol. V (1900), pp. 186 ff.

[12] See 'Relación Histórica de los Sucesos de la Rebelión de José Gabriel Tupac Amarú en las Provincias del Perú, el año de 1780', p. 23, in Pedro de Angelis, op. cit.

same year, with a break of one month in July due to the arrival of relief forces. The relief column was unable to provide any support to the besieged city, and was forced to leave again at the beginning of August.

5. Further to the north, in what was the corregimiento of Larecaja, Andrés Mendigure was active. He was also known as Andrés Tupac Amarú, nephew of José Gabriel. He was, perhaps, the most brilliant military leader of the rebels. It was under his leadership that the rebels captured the town of Sorata, an important event in the history of the uprisings.

6. Revolts broke out in two further areas: that of Chayanta, which has been mentioned before, and that of the neighbouring region of Cochabamba.

Although Tupac Catari (Julian Apaza) had been captured and executed by the middle of November 1781, and Diego and Andrés were holding talks in order to reach an agreement with the authorities, uprisings and revolts continued until June 1782, especially in the areas round La Paz.[13]

It must again be emphasized that these revolts were extremely bloody. The following descriptions, taken from the diary of Segurola, afford us an idea of what happened:[14]

Reference cannot be made to the outrages and cruelties committed by our enemies on our people, both on those captured alive and on the corpses left behind on the battlefield, without the greatest pain, horror and compassion, as it was common for them to show their anger against the Spaniards by cutting off heads, arms, legs, and by peeling strips of skin from the bodies, dancing around the corpses whenever they found any.

[13] Modern accounts of the course of the rebellions may be found in Boleslao Lewin, op. cit., in Daniel Valcarcel, La Rebelión de Tupac Amarú (Mexico: Fondo de Cultura Económica, 1947), and in Lilian Estelle Fisher, The Last Inca Revolt (Oklahoma: University of Oklahoma Press, 1966). For descriptions contemporary to the events, see Segurola's diary; also 'Relación histórica de los sucesos de la rebelión de José Gabriel Tupac Amarú en las provincias del Perú', in Pedro de Angelis, Colección de Obras y Documentos para la historia antigua y moderna de las provincias del Río de la Plata (Buenos Aires, Editorial Lajouane, 2nd ed., 1910, Vol. IV, pp. 275–398). Another very detailed contemporary account is the account already referred to: 'Relación de los hechos más notables acaecidos en la sublevación general fraguada en los reinos del Perú, por el Indio José Gabriel Tupac Amarú, gobernador del pueblo de Tungasuca en la provincia de Tinta, que asociado de otros sus secuaces, causó horrorosos estragos desde el año 1780, hasta el de 1782 en que se reprimió el orgullo de la conjuración', published in Revista de Archivos y Bibliotecas Nacionales (Lima), año III, Vol. V (1900), pp. 143–298.

[14] 'Diario', i, p. 66. The last entry of this diary is dated 1 July 1781 in La Paz.

Another description from a different source refers to strife in the Puno area in the following terms:

'After the squads of cavalry mentioned above had left it (meaning Chucuito), the Indians entered, and as they encountered no resistance they committed unparalleled atrocities on our men. They killed more than 400 Spaniards and half-castes of both sexes, without sparing even babes at the breast.

'Almost simultaneously, the Indians of this other part of Azangaro and Lampa (two corregimientos situated northwest of Lake Titicaca), redoubling their efforts, again attacked the village of Capachica of this province (Capachica is a town on Titicaca facing the town of Puno), whose loyal Indians, with a few half-breeds (*mestizos*), had at first repulsed them; but in the end, the greater numbers of the foe prevailed, and all Spaniards and white men (*gente blanca*) who were caught were stabbed to death.

'Thus the only Spaniards left in this vicinity are those who managed to save themselves in the town (*en la Villa*, i.e. Puno) which now constitutes a small island of happiness in the midst of a sea of rebellion.'[15]

This 'small island of happiness' was also to be lost shortly afterwards. The report was written by a chronicler who was highly critical of the Spanish administration and put all the blame for the uprising on the misbehaviour of the corregidores. It was dated 28 April 1781, in Puno. Puno was abandoned by its defenders on 26 May.

These violent characteristics of the revolts are very significant. They constitute a striking contrast to the often repeated description of the Indian as a submissive, patient, and docile person. This image was already developed in the sixteenth-century chronicles, and remained a conspicuous feature of eighteenth-century accounts.[16] This behaviour of the Indians contained many apparent contradictions: an incapacity to assert their most minimal rights shifted abruptly into rapine, savagery, robbery, and other forms of violence during the period of the local revolts and the more extensive outbreaks of 1780.

[15] From 'Relación Histórica de los Sucesos de la Rebelión de José Gabriel Tupac en las provincias del Perú', de Angelis, op. cit. (2nd ed.), pp. 395–6.

[16] E.g. the famous 'Secret Report' written by Jorge Juan and Antonio de Ulloa in the 1740s. They describe Indians as being easily handled and exploited, even by negro slaves: *Noticias Secretas de América*, 2nd Part, Chapters I, II, III, and IV. A similar subservient attitude is described by Fray Rodrigo de Loayza in a document written two centuries earlier. He points out how the Indians were abused, insulted, and exploited by their own chiefs, and how they humbly accepted this abuse. 'Memorial de las cosas del Pirú tocantes a los Indios' (Madrid, 1586), printed in *Colección de Documentos Ineditos para la Historia de España* (Madrid, 1889), p. 587.

III

It is now necessary to examine the nature of Peruvian society in order to place the events of the rebellion in a broader framework.

Much has been said about Spain's enlightened despotism. It is not out intention to discuss its nature in eighteenth-century Spain itself; whatever one may think of the degree of transformation accomplished in that country, it is most important to remember that the uprising in Peru occurred at the very time when the modernizing measures of the monarchy were at their peak during the reign of Charles III (1759–88). Administrative reforms had already been introduced by the first Bourbon king, Philip V (1700–46), and his successor Ferdinand VI (1746–59); but it was with Charles III and his group of brilliant ministers, civil servants, and men of letters like Aranda, Floridablanca, Campomanes, Jovellanos, Cabarrus, Olavide, José de Galvez, that this trend reached its climax.[17]

The Caroline projects for industrial growth, bureaucratic efficiency, the strengthening of military potential, are well known. In the case of Peru, they involved profound changes, both in the structure of Peruvian society and in the relations of Peru with other regions of the empire.

Even as late as the 1770s, Lower Peru and its urban core, Lima, still occupied a strategic position in the Spanish empire, partly as a source of revenue for the Crown and partly as the commercial centre which supplied the mining regions of Upper Peru (Bolivia). But this position had increasingly deteriorated throughout the eighteenth century. What the Peruvian commercial interests wanted, especially those of Lima, was to control the supply of goods to the mines as well as the marketing of metal production in the Charcas area.[18] The Charcas silver mines supplied half the total production of the viceroyalty and stimulated a great variety of commercial activities which constituted a source of wealth to the Lima merchants. These benefits were severely menaced by the fact that Lima was no longer the cheapest port for the importation of European goods for the Charcas or the Chilean market,

---

[17] The viceroys in Peru of the Caroline administration were Superunda (1745–61), Amat (1761–76), Guirior (1776–80), Jauregui (1780–4), and Croix (1784–90). For the part played by José de Galvez's career, see Herbert Ingram Priestly, *José de Galvez, Visitor-General of New Spain, 1765–1771* (Berkeley, 1916). For the social, political, and economic events in Spain itself in the later part of the eighteenth century, see R. Carr, *Spain* (Oxford: Clarendon Press, 1966), pp. 60–78.

[18] What is now Bolivia was alternatively known as Upper Peru or Charcas.

nor for the export of metal from the Upper Peruvian mines. In earlier centuries, this had been so because Lima could take advantage of the basic social investment made in the Inca empire. However, this advantage was now fading away. The introduction of goods through the port of Buenos Aires was cheaper for two reasons: safer maritime and cheaper terrestrial routes.

With the benefit of its existing privileges, Lima was able to manage quite well, though it was always threatened by the merchants of Buenos Aires, who were ready to use every legitimate, or illegitimate, means to exploit their natural advantages. When Charles III decided to create the new viceroyalty of the Río de la Plata on 1 August 1776, Lima interests were very adversely affected. Now Upper Peru was to come under the jurisdiction of Buenos Aires, with all the economic consequences implied by this decision.[19]

Those interests concerned with the importation of European goods and the export of minerals were damaged most. Those connected with the production of local goods, especially coarse fabrics for the consumption of the popular classes, apparently continued to trade with the Charcas area without being so disastrously hit by the creation of the new viceroyalty.[20]

The Crown was primarily concerned with strategic considerations when the viceroyalty was created. Above all, it wanted to consolidate the position in the Río de la Plata region, thus eliminating the threat of the Portuguese, and preparing against the more formidable danger of the British. The Spaniards marshalled all their available resources in order to finance their expedition against the Portuguese occupying Rio Grande and Colonia del Sacramento on the other side of the River Plate, facing Buenos Aires. Thus, in addition to her loss of the Upper Peruvian market, Lima was also left with grave financial burdens

---

[19] The whole process is very aptly described in Cespedes del Castillo, op. cit.

[20] This may be seen in the table worked out by Cañete which describes the quantity and types of products consumed in Potosí around 1790. The principal and almost only supplier of coarse textiles (bayetas de obraje) was Cuzco, while Buenos Aires supplied goods from Europe. (Cf. Marie Helmer, 'Documents pour l'histoire économique de l'Amérique du Sud. Commerce et industrie au Perou; a la fin du XVIIIme siècle', Revista de Indias, X, p. 522-4). Data of a similar nature were given by Viedma in 1788. The most important supplier of coarse textiles to Cochabamba was Cuzco. For this kind of textiles, no other important source of supply is mentioned. Cf. Francisco de Viedma, Descripción Geográfica y Estadística de la Provincia de Santa Cruz de la Sierra (Cochabamba, 1788), printed in Pedro de Angelis, Colección de Obras y Documentos Relativos a la Historia Antigua y Moderna de las Provincias del Río de la Plata, iii, pp. 101-2, 105.

by her obligation to support the war effort. Other serious financial expenditure was incurred after the local victory over the Portuguese as a consequence of the war which from April 1779 Spain was to wage with Britain for four years.

The Crown gave special powers to her envoy, the visitor-general José Antonio de Areche in June of the year following the creation of the viceroyalty of Río de la Plata, in order to strengthen the viceroyalties of Peru and Buenos Aires. He was a stern, severe, and devoted official, typical of the new class of career men who had linked their destinies with the fortunes of the Caroline administration. He was to become one of the most important actors in the dramatic events that took place between the years 1780 and 1883. Areche's appointment, as were those of Galvez in Mexico and Escobedo who succeeded him in Peru, was part of the government's plan for completely renewing and reshaping the colonial administration. He was also closely connected with the introduction of the Intendant System, which was to follow shortly afterwards.

IV

We must now examine the various sectors of colonial society in Peru.

The upper class of the colony included high-ranking state officials, viceroy, *oidores* (judges of the audiencia), Treasury officials, corregidores, and governors. Also in the upper classes were influential Church dignitaries, as well as military commanders. Merchants were very important in this sector of society; as in many other parts of the Spanish empire, their financial resources made them powerful. The administration often had to seek their aid when its financial problems became acute. The documents relating to their activities show that a few of them bore titles of nobility.[21]

There was in Lima a decaying social sector which owed its origins to the first settlers and *conquistadores*. By the early part of the eighteenth

[21] For instance, among the names of the two rival lists competing for the positions of prior and consuls for the consulado or guild merchant in Lima in 1748 elections, only two titles of nobility are mentioned in a list about fifty names long. *A.G.I.* Audiencia de Lima, Legajo 1545. Many of the lists in the same Legajo show the same feature. Titles of nobility in America were generally not of high standing, and the holders of the most valued titles remained in the peninsula. Cf. Richard Konetzke 'Die Enstehung des Adels in Hispanisch Amerika während der Kolonialzeit', *Vierteljahrschrift für Sozial-und Wirtschaft & geschichte*, B.39, pp. 215–50, and Guillermo Lohmann Villena, *Los Americanos en las ordenes nobiliarias* (1529–1900) (Madrid, 1942). Pp. I–LXXIX.

century their descendants had become large-landed proprietors in the valleys of the coastal regions. Landowners were a distinguished body, constituting the main element of provincial society. Many were absentee proprietors, living permanently in Lima. Their style of life was magnificent and lavish. However, after the 1687 earthquakes, and those that followed in 1701, 1720, and 1764, their means of livelihood were adversely affected. Moreover, wheat production in the coastal valleys was interrupted by a blight which destroyed the grain.

The economic situation of this class was deteriorating, although its members tried to maintain their former way of life as far as possible.[22] Many of them had titles of nobility of various kinds, often in the form of membership of orders of chivalry; they constituted a sort of local court for the viceroyalty. Through their local connections they tried to obtain positions in the local bureaucracy, and very often they became connected through marriage to the enriched class of merchants.[23] They formed a notorious pressure group, as Areche became acutely aware as soon as he arrived in Lima. They were the main force behind the conflict which developed between Viceroy Guirior and the visitor-general Areche.[24]

In the towns of the interior, the composition of the local ascendancy was similar, although merchants, nobility, and bureaucrats were less important than they were in Lima. To these, other groups must be added: the mine-owners and the owners of textile factories. The mine-owners resided near the mining sites; Pasco, Oruro, Cailloma, Carangas, Potosí, Huancavelica, are examples, but there were many small mining sites scattered around the large centres. Mining was never undertaken with large amounts of capital nor with advanced technology during the eighteenth century; the main innovations had been introduced in the sixteenth and seventeenth centuries. By 1750 mining production in Peru and Upper Peru was passing through very difficult times, although conditions varied from place to place.[25] The relative importance of Pasco had grown vis-à-vis the other mining

[22] Cespedes del Castillo, op. cit., p. 724.

[23] Cf. Lohmann Villena, Los Americanos en las Ordenes Nobiliarias, p. LVIII.

[24] This is very well described by Vicente Palacio Atard, 'Areche y Guirior—Observaciones sobre el proceso de una visita al Perú', Anuario de Estudios Americanos, III, pp. 291 ff.

[25] Cespedes del Castillo, op. cit., p. 748, and Modesto Bargalló, La Minería y la Metalurgia en la América Española durante la época colonial (Mexico: Fondo de Cultura Económica, 1955), pp. 241, 299.

sites, while Huancavelica and Oruro were experiencing great hardship,[26] and the condition of Potosí wes also deteriorating.[27]

The social status of the mine-owners was ambiguous. Their prestige was at a low ebb, and many believed that they were inefficient, lazy, and incapable of introducing the necessary innovations for increasing output. Their capacity to meet their financial obligations was also seriously questioned. A letter by a mine-owner to the periodical *Mercurio Peruano* reflects the resentment of this group:[28]

'The enemies of the trade try to justify themselves by saying that the miner is a *swindler* [in italics in the original document], a *defaulter* [also in italics], and a *wastrel*. I will reply to these charges one by one. I do not deny that amongst us, as in all other sectors of society, there exist a few charlatans and cheats; and that despite the vigilance of authorities we have had a few despicable additions to our ranks; but it is grossly unfair that because of a few sinners so many innocents should suffer. . . . The last objection that we are a lot of wastrels. . . . Miners are men who ride on a mule from sunrise to sunset, eternally loaded with a miserable *poncho*, nourished generally with potatoes and mutton, who live in huts that seem more like ferret holes than the living quarters of rational beings, who are continually exposed to snow, cold and the heat of the sun. 'The same passions which in the city absorb a fortune, such as greed and harlotry, in a miner are paid for with a sack of potatoes and a length of English flannel.'

These difficulties, combined with the risks of investing in mining ventures, made money increasingly costly for the mine-owners. Their debts to merchants and other financiers grew. In the same letter quoted above, an annual interest rate of 72 per cent was given as the normal rate for money lent for mining, and in addition legal guarantees to back the loans were also demanded:[29]

'The Kingdom of Mexico has always flourished because of its mines: Peru, whose mines are richer and more plentiful, barely supports herself with them.

[26] By 1774 Oruro and Pasco each were producing about a third of Potosí's output. Cf. Manuel de Amat y Junient, *Memoria de Gobierno*, Publicaciones de la Escuela de Estudios Hispano–Americanos (Sevilla, 1947), p. 257. In 1720 the revenue of the Treasury in Pasco was only 10 per cent of that of Oruro. Cf. Michèle Colin, *Le Cuzco, à la fin du XVIIe et au début du XVIIIe siècle* (Paris, 1966), p. 210. For Huancavelica cf. Arthur Preston Whitaker, *The Huancavelica Mercury Mines* (Cambridge, Harvard University Press, 1941), chapters III to VII.

[27] Amat pointed out that during the administration of Viceroy Esquilache (1615–21) consumption of mercury for the production of silver was more than twice as much as it was in his time. See Amat, op. cit. p. 258.

[28] *Mercurio Peruano*, No. 3, 9 de enero de 1791, fol. 21.

[29] *Mercurio Peruano*, No. 3, 9 de enero de 1791, fol. 21, 22, 23.

There a merchant, a rich man, on the mere word of a miner, invests in the mine 50 or 100 thousand pesos and does not flinch when he hears that an error has been made with the vein: here whenever an investor lends some 10 or 12 thousand pesos (if any do reach such an amount), he wants to put the miner and the mines in a vice . . . and to have his gains without any losses. . . . Nature sometimes fools them (the miners), and at other times they are tyrannised by the cruelty of men. Amongst the latter, the suppliers take first place.'

It was impossible to solve the problem of the decline of mining production, since it stemmed from the fact that the richest veins were already exhausted, while the exploitation of the poorer ores demanded technology and capital that were not available. Efforts on the part of the Governments and private individuals to introduce the necessary innovations were not lacking,[30] and these were intensified during the 1780s through the creation by Visitor-General Escobedo of the *Tribunal de Minería*, and the arrival of the Nordenflicht mission of mining experts, to investigate and determine the most appropriate mining techniques.

One chronicler described the economic conditions in Oruro as especially desperate:

'For ten years the work in the mines has fallen back alarmingly; thus there is not one now that is really under way, or that brings its owner in enough to maintain it and keep it going. This was the only activity which supported the area: the complete breakdown of the mines placed the miners in an appalling situation, so much so that those who were amongst the most important, and who in the past had possessed huge incomes . . . found themselves in dire poverty, heavily in debt, and unable to pay their bills either to the King or to private individuals, or to continue with their work. The suppliers refused all further deliveries.'[31]

Owners of textile mills also constituted an important part of the population. Their activity rose to its peak in the last decades of the seventeenth century. One source estimates that there were about 300 factories in the area now known as Peru. These textile factories were called *obrajes*.

[30] See for instance Viceroy Guirior's comments in his 'Memoria de Gobierno' in *Relaciones de los Virreyes y Audiencias que han gobernado el Perú* (Madrid, 1872), iii, pp. 25–6. See also the very elaborate proposals on mining techniques made by Juan Carlos García de Avila, priest in Guayllate (Cochabamba) in 1786, *Real Academia de la Historia* (Madrid) (Colección Mata Linares), Vol. 5, f. 334–423.

[31] 'Relación histórica de los sucesos de la rebelión de José Gabriel Tupac–Amarú' in De Angelis, op. cit., p. 282.

In the century that followed, their importance declined and they specialized only in the cheapest type of clothes (called *ropa de la tierra*), as they were unable to compete with those of better quality produced in Europe. In the bishopric of Cuzco, there was a large concentration of factories of varying sizes (some of them, known as *chorrillos*, were small and organized on a family basis). Some textile factories employed large numbers of workers, in a few cases as many as a thousand.[32] As we have already mentioned, Cruzco was a net exporter to Upper Peru of textiles of this coarse type, a part of it coming from other regions of Peru, and also from Quito.

IV

At the other end of the social spectrum we find the Indians. They formed the bulk of the labour force for the mines and foundries, while they also constituted an important, although not an exclusive, sector of the working force in the textile factories.

The supply of Indian labour for the mines was obtained through the *mita* system. Under this system, the Indians in certain provinces were obliged to work in the mines for a period of three months every seven years. Altogether, the Indian had to remain in the mine for a year, resting for two weeks after a full week's work. The main centre of employment was Potosí in 1750, and there about 3,000 Indians were recruited by the mita system.[33] Sixteen provinces were supposed to provide *mitayos* (mita wokers) to the mines and the foundries of Potosí.

Regulations on mita obligations were issued in 1574 by Viceroy Toledo.[34] A census was completed at that time which included about 100,000 male adult Indians of between the ages of 18 and 50. The sixteen selected provinces had to provide 13,500 Indians yearly; 4,500 of them would be working at the same time at Potosí. However, because of the decline in population in the provinces selected as suppliers of mita labour, the quantity sent to Potosí diminished

[32] Silva Santisteban, *Los Obrajes en el Virreynato del Perú* (Publicaciones del Museo Nacional de Historia, Lima, 1964), p. 161.

[33] Viceroy Superunda (1746-61) gave a total of 2,900 for the middle of the eighteenth century. See 'Relación que escribe el Conde de Superunda, Virrey del Perú . . .' in *Memorias de los Virreyes que han gobernado al Perú durante el tiempo del Coloniaje Español*, iv (Lima: Bailly, 1859).

[34] For a wide range of regulations concerning Indian labour, see *Ordenanzas del Virrey Toledo* in Roberto Levillier (ed.) *Gobernantes del Perú* (Madrid, 1924), viii, p. 419. For the process of concentration of Indians in *reducciones*, see R. Levillier, *Don Francisco de Toledo* (Madrid: Espasa-Calpe, 1935), i, pp. 246 ff.

constantly. Although mine owners made several attempts to extend mita obligations to other provinces, the vice-regal authorities were reluctant to follow suit.[35]

The mita system was presumably based on a traditional procedure of the Inca regime; but its introduction under the Spanish administration gave rise to several profound consequences.

In the first place, the actual conditions of work in the mines were very harsh. The 'black legend' of Spanish colonization repeats that the mines were graveyards; that most of the Indians entered them never to return. Population estimates from 1500 onwards show that the Indian community declined; but this decline appears to have been steepest between 1531 and 1561. The first colonial census of 1561 registered a population of 1,106,672, whereas estimates of the population under the previous Inca rule fluctuate between 2 and 10 million. Even if the 2 million figure is accepted, the rate of reduction was very sharp and much greater than that which followed, when the colonial regime was stabilized and the mita system enforced. The lowest population point was reached in 1754, with a total of 350,000. After that, it increased again at quite a rapid pace, almost doubling in the following forty years.[36]

The early decline in the Indian population appears to have been caused by the advent of diseases and plagues. Working conditions in the mines were harmful, but critics of the regime perhaps exaggerate. It was common for free labour to work in the mines, and for the mitayos to engage themselves as free labour during their rest periods, or on weekends.

From an economic point of view, the mita system in the eighteenth century was a device to cheapen cost of labour. The cost of a free labourer was seven pesos a week, and for this wage the supply of labour was sufficient to cover demand. On the other hand, the salary paid to the mitayo was only three pesos a week.

Mine-owners emphasized repeatedly that they were unable to keep the mines running with costs as high as those demanded by the employment of free labourers.[37] Given the technology in use in Upper

[35] See 'Relación que escribe el Conde de Superunda . . .' p. 89, where he refers to a decree of 12 October 1732 against mine-owners' demands.

[36] See David Noble Cook, 'La Población en el Perú Colonial', *Anuario de Estudios de Investigaciones Históricas*, No. 8, 1965 (Rosario, Universidad Nacional del Litoral), p. 93.

[37] See for instance 'Extracto del memorial ajustado tomado en el Consejo de Indias sobre mitas y si se debe quitar', Colección Mata Linares, Vol. 38, f. 18.

Peru, free labour costs seemed to be very high; all attempts to increase productivity through technological innovations failed.

This may have been due to the lack of entrepreneurial spirit on the part of the mine-owners, which contrasts with the inventiveness of their forefathers in the sixteenth century, or that of their contemporaries in Mexico. But probably it was simply a hard fact of Peruvian silver mining that it could not pay for its costs given the price of labour and its productivity.[38]

A most important consequence of the mita was the migration it brought about in the Indian population. The significant element here was that a high proportion of Indians did not return to their places of origin. They remained near the working sites, employing themselves as miners, in service, or wandered from place to place engaged in the most diverse types of activities. In 1680, Ibarra estimated that a total of twenty-four thousand displaced persons were living in Potosí.[39] Migration was a consequence not only of the movement of labour to the mines but was also due to the desire of the Indians to evade their obligations. Many of them migrated to avoid working in the mines.

The status of these migratory Indians was often ambiguous. They were generally referred to as 'foreign Indians'. They settled in villages, in towns, or went to zones not yet under the control of the Spanish administration, across the frontier of colonial culture. In the censuses they appear as *indios forasteros*, although sometimes they were classified as *yanaconas*.[40] Registration of 'foreign' Indians was very irregular. They tried as much as they could to evade poll-tax, and thus were often not entered in the censuses; it is clear that the 'foreign' Indians' population was greater than that recorded in the censuses.

On the other hand, constant conflicts arose on the question of forcing foreign Indians to fulfil mita obligations. Many migratory Indians were not registered, so it was not necessary for them to go to the

[38] It has been pointed out by Maiguashca that after Independence, between 1820 and 1830, there was a big influx of British miners to Peru, attracted by the widely held belief as to the inefficiency of Peruvian mine-owners, on the assumption that they could succeed where others had failed. But things proved to be otherwise, because most of them had gone by the beginning of the 1840s. See Juan Maiguashca, 'A Reinterpretation of the Guano Age, 1840–1880', unpublished D.Phil. thesis (Oxford, 1967), p. 18.

[39] See Guillermo Lohmann Villena, *El Conde de Lemos*.

[40] Pedro Vicente Cañete y Dominguez—*Gúia Histórica, Geográfica, Física, Política, Civil y Legal del Gobierno e Intendencia de la Provincia de Potosí, año 1791* (La Paz, 1952), p. 386.

mita.[41] Many worked for Spanish landowners or townspeople, classifying themselves as yanaconas. As Matienzo defined them, the yanaconas were those Indians who had abandoned their birthplaces to live as servants among the Spaniards;[42] as such, they were exempt from mita and tax burdens. The term was already vague in the eighteenth century, and often foreign Indians without land were simply called yanaconas. Irrespective of the term that may be used to classify them, the rootless and floating migratory Indian came to form an increasing proportion of the population.[43]

Whether or not they were registered by the tax collectors, foreign Indians could often avoid the mita, in spite of the fact that mine-owners were always putting pressure on the authorities to include more Indians, in addition to the 'original Indians', in the levies, as they attempted to extend the obligation to provinces other than the original sixteen.

They were not very successful. For example, Viceroy Count of Superunda, when asked in the 1750s to enforce a 1732 law which decreed that foreign Indians must work as mitayos, commented:

'The decree stating that foreign Indians must also comply with mita regulations was a novelty, the introduction of which demanded much caution. As it is against tradition, it might produce some disturbance, and undoubtedly it was this fact above all others which prevented its implementation, because when I took office no provision had been made to force foreigner Indians to render this service. But the Potosí miners, looking only to their own profit, and not fearing the consequences of their actions, persuaded Don Ventura Santelices (the highest official in Potosí) to enforce the decreee; and although it was declared that settled Indians possessing land should work as mitayos in the same way as the original ones, they protested legally against it, and they were successful . . . and . . . I resolved by a decree of August 26, 1752, that in the provinces contributing to the mita of Potosí . . . foreign Indians including

---

[41] See Pedro Francisco Arismendi, 'Informe del Subdelegado de Porco sobre la mita de Ursainqui, Abril 29, 1790'. Colección Mata Linares, Vol. 37, f. 132–3.

[42] Juan de Matienzo, *Gobierno del Perú 1567* (Travaux de l'Institut Français d'Études Andines, Paris–Lima, 1967), p. 25.

[43] 'Indians are not any more under the control of their caciques and curacas and concentrated in "ayllus" and "parcialidades" as when Toledo numbered them, but are scattered and dispersed', complained Viceroy Duke de la Palata in 1689 in a letter to the King. In the census ordered by this Viceroy, of the 64,581 registered Indians in the sixteen mita provinces, 31,378 were foreigners and 16,000 lived sheltered in Spanish estates. See Alberto Crespo Rodas, 'La Mita de Potosí', *Revista Histórica* (Lima), Vol. XII (1955–6), pp. 158–62.

those without land, but settled, should be listed in the censuses as demanded by the mine owners, excluding vagrant foreigner Indians. . . .'[44]

As is implied by the quotation, some displaced Indians were able to obtain land after settling in a community. Others remained attached to the communities but did not possess land. Authorities classified them in the censuses as 'foreign Indians with land' and 'foreign Indians without land' (*forasteros con tierras*, and *forasteros sin tierras*). Others presumably rendered some services to Spaniards and were registered as yanaconas. And still others were not registered at all, and remained unattached, as a permanently vagrant population.

Many contemporary chroniclers described the behaviour of the displaced Indians. Although they designated them vaguely as foreign Indians, they were probably referring to the least integrated strata. They pointed to their disorganized and erratic behaviour. Let us quote, for instance, Cañete, who described the consequences of the displacements produced by the mita obligations:

'With all this (the mita), the unhappy Indians cannot find the relief which the King wishes them to have . . . because during the time that the mita lasts, they themselves and their families spend much more on their keep than they can earn. Consequently, they are in debt and when they leave this has to be paid off, so that they are poorer than before; and forced to beg or steal or to hide in the town, to get jobs as domestics or *minga* (that is to say, to work as free labourers) . . . and as the Indian's ruling passion is to be free, *he never returns home*, nor has he the means to do so, because all he earns he squanders on his vices and drunkenness.'[45]

Feyjoo de Sosa, chief accountant of the Treasury in Lima, describes the behaviour of Indian foreigners in much the same way, in 1778:

'I have been told that all the Indians in this capital are foreigners, as this same fact has been observed in the cities of Cuzco, Arequipa and Potosí. These migrations have caused them to become vagrants and nomads, and consequently the provinces remain deserted and unpopulated. . . . To prove what I have just said, the following reflections are offered. The original Indians (*originarios*) are called thus not because they all live in the ruined villages, but on the *haciendas*, mills, and ranches, surrounded by their wives and children, and the foreign Indians are those who go to provinces which are remote an

[44] See 'Relación que escribe el Conde de Superunda', pp. 90–1.
[45] Pedro Vicente Cañete y Dominguez, *Guía Histórica, Geográfica, Física, Política, Civil y Legal del Gobierno e Intendencia de la Provincia de Potosí, año 1791* (La Paz, 1952), p. 107.

strange to them, seeking help and a living; so that it can be seen that these people (*nación*) live as vagrants and nomads, wanderers in their land.'[46]

As a consequence of the decision of Viceroy Superunda to include foreign Indians in the mita, a census was carried out in 1754, under the direction of José de Orellana. Statistics are very significant. Of the total of 140,000 adult male Indians registered, 55,000 were foreigners, which represents about 40 per cent of the registered male Indian adults.[47] During Amat's viceroyalty, about twenty years later, another count gave a total of 172,000 adult male Indians with a very similar proportion between 'original' and 'foreign' Indians.[48] In addition, regional distribution varied widely. While in the departments of La Paz and Chuquisaca, the proportion of foreigners reached 60 per cent (the two departments covering approximately the present territory of Bolivia) in the department of Cuzco the proportion was 40 per cent and in Trujillo in northern Peru it was as low as 20 per cent.

V

In the local hierarchy, *caciques* or *curacas* had a socially strategic role. They were chieftains of Indian or mestizo origin, playing much the same role as they had in the Inca empire. With the collapse of the centralized government of the Inca empire, their power was greatly increased, and they became small lords in their area of influence. Many officials of the Inca regime at that time disguised themselves as curacas. As soon as the Spanish administration could consolidate its power, it limited the influence of these curacas severely. In this sphere, Viceroy Toledo developed the necessary legal instruments with which to do this through his regulations for corregidores.[49]

The fundamental tasks of the curacas involved the collection of poll-tax and the numbering and registering of Indians for the mita (in those provinces in which mita was practised). They had also some minor judicial power. Furthermore, curacas were exempt from tribute and mita, and received a salary. The position of curaca also implied privileges in land and water use.[50]

[46] See 'Parecer que dió Don Miguel Feyjo de Sosa . . .' Biblioteca Nacional (Madrid) MS. 13368, f. 30 and 30 v.

[47] *Memorias de los Virreyes que han gobernado al Perú*, iv, *Estadolos o Documentos* . . . Appendix x, 15.

[48] Amat, *Memoria de Gobierno*, p. 236.

[49] See Guillermo Lohmann Villena, *El Corregidor de Indios en el Perú bajo los Austrias* (Madrid: Ediciones Cultura–Hispánica, 1957), pp. 50–60.

[50] For an illustration of the opportunities for land monopoly given by the position of Curaca, see 'Relaciones de la Visita del Intendente de Arequipa Don

Indians of noble origin had preferential rights in competing for the position of curaca. In a royal degree of 1697, this fact was clearly stated '. . . (to) the caciques . . . as distinct from the Indians of lower status I leave the chieftainship with the name of Cacicazgo, to be inherited by the eldest son in each generation; cases concerning them are not to be brought before ordinary legal courts without knowledge of the Audiencias'.[51] By the 1770s, there were about 2,300 curacas in the Viceroyalty of Peru, representing 1·5 per cent of tributary Indians.

Added to their formal prerogatives, the caciques established a set of informal paternalistic relations over their region of influence. Tax collection and evasion depended on them. Not uncommonly, caciques engaged in business activities, as was the case with José Gabriel Tupac Amarú. They were clearly closely involved in the Spanish colonial system, and the frequent lawsuits between Indians concerning rights of *cacicazgo* show that the office involved prestige and power.

VI

At this point, some brief reference must be made to the Indian community's political and kinship structure: remnant of the previous Inca empire, it had integrated itself into the Spanish colonial culture, although it is not clear how far these residues of the older culture were still alive in the eighteenth century. On the other hand, scholars disagree on what was the real history and social structure of the previous Inca empire.[52]

Documents of the late eighteenth century reveal that Indians

Antonio Alvarez y Jimenes (1793–1796)' in Victor M. Barriga, *Memorias para la historia de Arequipa* (Arequipa, 1948), ii, p. 12.

[51] Reproduced in Richard Konetzke, *Colección de Documentos para la historia de la formación social de Hispanoamérica, 1493–1800*, III. I, 1691–1779 (Madrid, 1962), p. 67. 'R.C. que se considere a los descendientes de caciques como nobles de su raza', Madrid, 26 Mar. 1697.

In regard to legal rights and obligations of caciques, see *Recopilación de leyes de los Reinos de las Indias mandados imprimir y publicar por la majestad católica del rey don Carlos II, nuestro señor*. 4 Vols. 5th ed. (Madrid, 1841), Libro VI, Título 7, Leyes I–XVII. Law II refers to the duty of Audiencias to protect the rights of Caciques; Law III to inheritance privileges; Law XIII relates to their judicial power.

[52] Reviewing Brundage's *Empire of the Inca*, Zuidema goes so far as to say: 'The only positive thing we know about the history of these people (the Inca civilization) is the date when the Inca were conquered by the Spaniards, everything else is speculation'. See R. T. Zuidema, *American Anthropologist*, Vol. 67 (1965), p. 176. See also the heated exchange of views about the question in *American Anthropologist*, Vol. 68 (1966), pp. 229–31.

considered themselves as belonging to groupings called *ayllus*. It is not possible to say if every Indian was attached to one of them, but a considerable proportion were. Because of the continuous migration, registration of Indians either in parishes or with the local authorities was defective; these faults and omissions also arose out of the desire of the caciques to collect the poll-tax for their own benefit.[53]

The exact nature of the ayllus is not known. Rowe describes it as, in theory, a kin group with a territorial basis and, again theoretically, endogamous. He traces its descent by the male line.[54]

There is another feature of the Inca civilization which was taken over by the Spaniards. Each Inca province was divided into two sections, or moieties, the 'upper' and the 'lower' (*Hanansaya* and *Hurinsaya*).[55] Each section had a chief. The chief of the Upper Moiety was called the 'first person' (*primera persona*), and that of the Lower Moiety the 'second person' (*segunda persona*). The chief of the Lower Moiety was subordinate to that of the Upper.[56] The Spanish administration organized the Indians under the same hierarchical system, a system which formally at least still survived in the later eighteenth

[53] Commenting on the new census ordered by him and on the increase of about 150,000 Indians over the 612,000 registered in the 1754 census, Viceroy Amat considered that one of the causes of the increase was a better control over the frauds and concealments of the corregidores and the curacas. See Amat, *Memoria de Gobierno*, p. 236.

[54] See John Howland Rowe, 'Inca Culture at the time of the Spanish Conquest', in Julian H. Stewart (ed.), *Handbook of South American Indians* (Washington, 1946), Vol. II, pp. 253–5. Hildebrando Castro Pozo in the same book gives a similar definition: 'Social and Economico–Political evolution of the Communities of Central Perú', pp. 483, 499.

These characteristics have been qualified by other scholars. Zuidema says, for instance: 'The ayllu was the group of all people who were descended from one particular ancestor. This formulation implies that in fact each group to which an individual was linked by father or mother could be considered as an ayllu. With the exception of certain rules concerning incest, each group could be considered as exogamous or as endogomous according to the specific situation involved'. R. T. Zuidema, *The Ceque System of Cuzco* (Leiden: E. J. Brill, 1964), p. 26, footnote 10. It is significant to point out that Tupac Amarú claimed his rights to government through maternal descent, his direct ancestry being from a daughter of the Inca Felipe Tupac Amarú.

[55] They are usually called 'moieties' among anthropologists, although perhaps they were not governed by the rules of definition and exchange functions such as given for instance in Robin Fox, *Kinship and Marriage* (Penguin Books, 1967), p. 182.

[56] See Rowe, op. cit., p. 263; George Kubler, 'The Quechua in the Colonial World', in Stewart (ed.) op. cit., p. 364, Juan de Matienzo, *Gobierno del Perú 1567*, p. 20.

century. In each Indian village, or territorial unit, there was a higher authority which was the 'cacique primera persona', a second-ranking one, the 'cacique segunda persona'. In addition, each ayllu had its 'principal'.[57]

The precise way in which lineage and kinship assigned individuals to ayllus, if indeed such a precise method ever existed, need not conern us. But a discussion of the relationship of these structures to the rebellions is relevant, especially where Indians belonged to different ayllus and hierarchical systems. There is enough evidence to assert that these elements surviving from the previous Inca structure, and the particular way in which they were amalgamated with Spanish culture, provided the base for the emergence of local leaderships in opposition to the Spanish administration.

This may be illustrated by the case of Chayanta. The conflict between the corregidor Alos, the wealthy mine-owner Manuel Alvarez Villarroel, and the priest of Macha, Gregorio José de Merlos, was notorious.[58]

Each of them enjoyed good relations, perhaps of a somewhat temporary nature, with local Indian chieftains. Alvarez Villarroel, for instance, supported Pascual Chura, an Indian chieftain who was involved in the fight against Corregidor Alos. He also complained about Pedro Caipa, cacique of Pocoata, who was considered loyal in 1780 by Alos. At the same time, Alvarez Villarroel was on good terms with the 'second person' of Pedro Caipa. On the other hand, Merlos, the priest of Macha, in conflict with both Alvarez Villarroel and Alos, supported Tomas Catari's demands against Alos.[59]

There is some evidence of conflicts between the 'first person' and the 'second person' caciques.[60] However, there were many instances where they worked together in harmony.[61]

[57] Sometimes the cacique was named alcalde mayor, with somewhat higher prerogatives. See Waldemar Espinoza Soriano, 'El Alcalde Mayor Indígena en el Virreynato del Perú', Anuario de Estudios Americanos (1960), 17, pp. 183–300.

[58] See letter from Pino Manrique to Areche, Plata, 19 October 1780: A.G.I., Audiencia de Charcas, Legajo 596.

[59] See 'Informe de Manuel Alvarez Villarroel, Plata, Octubre 14, 1780', A.G.I., Audiencia de Charcas, Legajo 596.

[60] For instance, the conflict between the cacique of Tacna, Toribio Ara, and his 'segunda' Cipriano Julian Quelopana, on the rights of cacicazgo. Cf. 'Relaciones de la Visita del Intendente de Arequipa . . .' op. cit. p. 10.

[61] In the turmoils of Quilaquila in December 1780, for instance, the cacique, Agustin Amuchuy, joined forces with Tomas Romero, his 'segunda', against foreign rebels. Cf. A.G.I., Indiferente General, Legajo 411, 'Cuaderno No. 2 del Auto por los Disturbios de Quilaquila'.

There appear to have been tension and clashes between the members of different ayllus. These strains weakened loyalties. This can be seen in the case of the murder of Florencio Lupa, cacique of the town of Moscari, which was attributed by some to members of another ayllus.[62]

One has to remember, when considering these cases, that membership of an ayllu implied rights to land and water, privileges that, as has been said before, were considerably increased when the position of cacique was attained.

VII

Among the members of the Spanish colonial establishment, we have mentioned the corregidor. He was a central figure in the system, and with the same name or that of 'alcalde mayor' existed throughout the entire Spanish empire. The corregidores had several functions, although some of them were not fully specified. In a very general way they were the representatives of the king in their provinces, and as such enjoyed considerable power.[63]

They were supposed to provide protection to the Indians. Previously this function had been carried out by another official, the protector of the Indians. But this position was abolished in the villages and only remained in existence in the towns.[64] A most important obligation was the collection of the poll-tax, and the organization of the sending of mitayos to the respective mines. All this was done with the help of the caciques.[65] In his province, everyone, whether Indian, mestizo, or Spaniard, was under jurisdiction of the corregidor. The corregidor could choose as site of residence any town or village in the province, which would then automatically become the capital of the corregimiento.

The introduction of the corregidor in Peru in the sixteenth century fulfilled several function. We have already mentioned those relevant

[62] Witnesses report that he was killed by members of the ayllu Sunichito which was not Lupa's own. See 'Cuadernos No. 10 de la Sublevación de Chayanta', *A.G.I.*, Audiencia de Charcas, Legajo 596.

[63] See Lohmann Villena, *Corregidor de Indios*, p. 222. Also J. M. Ots Capdequi, *Instituciones* (Barcelona, 1959), pp. 469–71.

[64] Lohmann Villena, *Corregidor de Indios*, p. 231.

[65] It should be pointed out that there were two kinds of corregidores, those of Indian villages and those of Spanish towns and cities. We are describing here the corregidor of Indians. But often the corregidor of Spanish towns had Indians under his jurisdiction, and so many of the features described here are applicable to him.

to the curacas. Another important aim of the Crown was to hinder the formation of a landed nobility in America, with rights of lordship over vassals. The corregidor thus represented a successful attempt to curb the growing power of the *encomendero*.[66]

There was another peculiarity of the corregidor which carried with it profound social consequences. Being a royal official, he received a salary which was related to the tax capacity of the province. Annual salaries of corregidores thus varied approximately between 1,200 and 4,800 pesos.[67] The corregidor was not allowed to practise trade or to engage in any kind of private commerce, and this was specifically included in the oath he had to take before occupying his post. These restrictions were envisaged to prevent conflicts with local traders.

But it was soon evident that with these salaries it was impossible to obtain efficient personnel for the task.[68] Corregidores were therefore allowed to practise the so-called *repartimiento* which afforded a monopoly of compulsory trade with the Indians of the villages. The corregidor was allowed to sell them a certain quantity of goods during his five-year period of office, and the Indians were compelled to buy them.

This procedure came to be increasingly criticized from almost every quarter of society. During their well-known voyage through South America, Juan and Ulloa bitterly condemned the practice.[69] One of the arguments against the repartimiento was that it really involved a way of getting rid of surplus goods. The goods which the Indians were forced to buy were of little use to them, and their price was considerably higher than the one they would have paid in the open market.

The repartimiento involved more than just the Indians and the

[66] See R. Konetzke, op. cit., p. 224.

[67] We are stating salaries in eight *reales* pesos. Salaries were usually expressed in the so-called *peso ensayado*, an imaginary unit valued approximately 65 per cent higher than the eight reales pesos (*peso de ocho reales* or *peso corriente*). Lohmann Villena gives the salaries of all the corregidores in Peru for the middle of the seventeenth century. See Lohmann Villena, *Corregidor de Indios*, pp. 595–600. These salaries were kept at the same level throughout the whole eighteenth century until the abolition of the position of corregidor. See *A.G.I.*, Audiencia de Lima, Legajos, 633–7. For the ratio between pesos de a ocho to pesos ensayados, see Michele Colin, op. cit., 'Conversions Monétaires'.

[68] See the expense budget of Manuel de Elcorrobarrutia, corregidor of Chancay. He estimates expenses for five years to be 59,700. Melchor de Paz, *Guerra Separatista* (Lima, 1952), ii, p. 307; see also the rather cynical defence of the corregidores made by the probable author of the famous *Lazarillo de Ciegos Caminantes*: Alonso Carrió de la Vandera, *Reforma del Perú* (Lima, 1966), pp. 30–1.

[69] Jorge Juan y Antonio de Ulloa, op. cit., pp. 198–9.

corregidor. Usually the corregidor obtained the goods on credit from merchants in the towns. Consequently, he became heavily in debt. As it was not always easy to collect money, given the permanent possibility of conflict, not many traders were prepared to run the necessary risks, and those that were charged higher interest rates.[70]

Leaving aside these distribution problems, the repartimiento was clearly a way of increasing consumption. It forced demand on a community whose living patterns and habits were only weakly connected to the Spanish market structure. Thus, the repartimiento system was supported not only by the corregidores but also by producers and certain groups of merchants. Fear of lowering the level of economic activity was a factor frequently considered in discussions on the abolition of the repartimiento.[71]

The Crown was clearly aware of the complications created by the practice of repartimiento. As its abolition would mean increasing expenses for the administration—because it would involve increasing the salaries of corregidores—the Crown introduced measures to check abuses. Each corregimiento was assigned a maximum number of pesos. The corregidor was not allowed to distribute goods among the Indians above that figure.[72] For instance, in the archbishopric of Lima, for a five-year period, the corregidor was allowed a *reparto* of 1,153,000 for a total adult male population of 45,000. This meant about 6 pesos a year per capita.

Many cases were brought by Indians against corregidores for excessive repartos.[73] But even if these abuses had not existed, one has to bear in mind that the whole system was geared to forcing demand patterns on a community which had different living and consumption habits and was reluctant to adopt other standards. It was only natural to expect opposition to such a system.[74]

The corregidor was also an obstacle to the Crown's desire to centralize and organize its bureaucracy on a more efficient basis.

[70] See for instance 'Representación de la Ciudad del Cuzco en el año de 1768 sobre excesos de Corregidores y Curas', in *Relaciones de los Virreyes y Audiencias que han gobernado el Perú*, iii. 212–14.

[71] See Alonso Carrió de la Vandera, op. cit., pp. 50–1. He complains of the negative effects brought about by the abrogation of the repartimiento.

[72] A list of the maximum amounts allowed for repartimiento in each of the provinces of Peru is given in Mendiburu, *Diccionario*, iv. pp. 456–7.

[73] See for instance 'Testimonio de los autos seguidos por los caciques Hilacatas del pueblo de Calacoto, Pvcia. de Pacages, contra el Justicia Mayor de ella . . .', A.G.I., Audiencia Charcas, Legajo 592.

[74] A copious literature has been devoted to these cultural clashes which have

C

Given the mixed character of the corregidor's revenues (part salary from the Crown, and part the product of his own entrepreneurial ability), he was increasingly at odds with the new career men of the administration.[75]

The preoccupation of the Crown with raising the standard of efficiency of the corregidores already appears in the last decades of the seventeenth century. The right to nominate them was taken from the viceroys and transferred exclusively to the *Consejo de Indias* in Spain itself. Viceroys complained about this measure.[76] But, as may be seen in their titles of appointment, it is only after the middle of the eighteenth century that the corregidor was considered as an official rather than as a source of revenue through the sale of office to him. After the accession of Charles III, no special payment was recorded in their titles, except for the normal payment called *media annata*.[77]

In spite of these efforts to integrate them into the bureaucratic system, the contradiction arising from the fact that they were not wholly dependent on Crown salaries proved to be an insurmountable obstacle. Because of this, their position had to be regulated with more care than that of other state officials. The corregidor was usually not a man from the ranks of bureaucracy; his nomination was only for five years. His appointment was essentially a short-term reward, and the possibility of his remaining within the administration afterwards depended on many factors difficult to assess.

Thus, the corregidor was the weakest link in colonial administration, and he was doomed to disappear. In fact, the corregidor was superseded by the Intendant, introduced into Peru in 1784. The implementation of the Intendant System throughout the Spanish empire took a long time, but towards the end of the 1770s it was clear to everybody that it would be adopted.[78]

Areche's appointment to Peru as visitor-general was linked with

---

many times been connected with messianism. See Yonina Talmon, 'Millenarian Movements', *Archives européennes de sociologie*, VII, 2 (1966), p. 164.

[75] '. . . giving the Judge the possibility of trade is the same as offering him the opportunity of being delinquent . . .', said Feyjoo de Sosa. Melchor de Paz, op. cit., ii. 333.

[76] See 'Relación del Estado de los Reinos del Perú que hace el Excmo. Señor don José Armendaris, Marqués de Castel–Fuerte . . .' in *Memorias de los Virreyes que han Gobernado el Perú* . . . , p. 58.

[77] Cf. appointment titles of corregidores in *A.G.I.*, Audiencia Lima, Legajos 633–7.

[78] Cf. John Lynch, *Administración General Española* (Buenos Aires, 1962), Ch. III, for a general description of its introduction in America.

this administrative reform. In his reports to the Crown, he severely attacked the office of corregidor and often recommended that the repartimiento should be extinguished.[79]

Thus, although the repartimiento was hastily abolished shortly after the outbreak of the rebellions, it was a decision which the Crown had already in mind.

The decade of the 1770s was further characterized by a wide set of measures, the main purpose of which was to increase the efficiency of the bureaucracy. As a consequence, Crown revenues were expected to become larger. But this was not the only goal in mind. It was also planned to limit the abuses practised by powerful local interest groups and to encourage production through careful legislation.

Better selection of personnel for positions in the bureaucracy was a natural prerequisite for such a purpose. We have mentioned that after the accession of Charles III a change was already visible in the nomination of corregidores. But this change was only a prelude. In spite of the stringent meaures taken to select them,[80] the government was not satisfied with the recruitment. That the corregidor in this sense was a relic of the old regime is proved by the fact that out of the 59 appointed subdelegates in 1784 in the viceroyalty of Peru when the Intendant System was introduced, only 9 had previously been corregidores.[81] Not one of the *intendentes* or *tenientes asesores* had been corregidor. In the case of the viceroyalty of Rio de la Plata, only 4 out of 39, in the list given by Lynch, had previously been corregidores.[82]

VII

In our description of the social and political structure of Peru and Upper Peru in the 1780s, a stage has been reached where an attempt may be made to combine the different components we have described into an explanation of the characteristics of the rebellions. Let us sum up the most distinctive features.

[79] Letter from Areche to Galvez, No. 195, Lima, 16 May 1780, *A.G.I.*, Indiferente General, Legajo 1713. It opens with the sentence: 'It is not easy or possible to improve the Government of the Provinces of Perú nor its Treasury as long as the chiefs or corregidores are merchants . . .'

[80] The Crown had no systematic procedure to select its bureaucracy, least of all corregidores. Connections with high officials in the Consejo de Indias was one of the surest ways to obtain a position. Military men were often offered a corregimiento as a reward for services in the army.

[81] See Manuel de Mendiburu, 'Relación de los primeros Subdelegados de partido (ho∕ Subprefectos) que hubo en el Perú.' *Diccionario*, IV. 458.

[82] Lynch, op. cit., pp. 273–81.

A markedly more efficient bureaucracy was being selected to fill positions in the administration of the viceroyalty. This bureaucracy was not more equipped to enforce the laws issued by the Crown but was bound to do so; its future depended on the capacity of the state to increase the level of revenues. All evidence points to an increase in efficiency. Division and specification of functions were intensified and, yet more significant, laws were enforced with renewed vigour.[83] This entailed a re-examination of the efficiency of the old local personnel and a threat to many that they might lose their positions.

The attempt to modernize the bureaucracy also implied a threat to the local power groups in each region. Mine-owners and traders had now to pay taxes, because the new bureaucrats were resolutely committed to exact them. The same threat held true for the corregidor. His role completely contradicted the new reforming trend. The corregidor also evoked the enmity of other sectors of society. Many had grievances against him: especially Indians because of the repartimiento. But, as we have said, these complaints were not only a consequence of the opportunities afforded for abuse; hostility to the repartimiento system was widespread, regardless of the degree of cynicism with which the corregidor enforced it, although of course it was exasperated by cases of evident corrupt practice. To quote, for instance, Viceroy Guirior in his Memoirs of Government':

'And although I have already made plain to Your Excellency the corruption induced by the present disorders of trade in the provinces . . . I see at the same time that there have always been repartimientos but they have not produced

---

[83] One might point for instance to the case of the collection of the *alcabala* (sales tax) in Cuzco. Until 1765 it was auctioned to private individuals. After that it came under the responsibility of the Royal Officials; see 'Ordenación de las cuentas de los Oficiales Reales de la Real Hacienda y Caja de la Ciudad de Cuzco, Tesorero Don Joseph de Toledo y Contador Don Mariano Maruri . . . en el año que corrió desde el 1° de Mayo de 1764 hasta el 30 de Abril de 1765', *A.G.I.*, Audiencia de Cuzco, Legajo 38. In 1773 the establishment of Customs Houses was decreed as a separate branch of the Administration. The decree was carried into effect in 1775 (*A.G.I.*, Audiencia de Cuzco, Legajo 39, Pliego 45).
The following data are illuminating in assessing the performance of the Aduana of Cuzco:

Year	Alcabala (pesos de a ocho, round figures)	
1767	16,022	(*A.G.I.*, Cuzco, Legajo 38)
1772	15,564	(*A.G.I.*, Cuzco, Legajo 39)
1776	21,608	(*A.G.I.*, Cuzco, Legajo 39)
1778	28,854	(*A.G.I.*, Cuzco, Legajo 40)
1779	38,658	(*A.G.I.*, Cuzco, Legajo 41)
1783	50,484	(*A.G.I.*, Cuzco, Legajo 41)

such troublesome and regrettable demonstrations. . . . On the contrary, I
find that they were . . . practised with evident moderation . . . in places where
the people's resentment reached such a high pitch'.[84]

That is to say, there was no clear-cut correlation between abuse in
the reparto and the riots it produced. It is to be expected here, as
everywhere else, that the introduction of alien patterns of work-
discipline and consumption in a community with its own modes of
living—often directed at mere subsistence—should produce a lasting
state of irritation.

Thus the corregidor, by his very role, was the inevitable target of
the antagonism of the Indian community.

On the other hand, for the typical bureaucrat, the corregidor was
not a state official but a trader in disguise. Resentment of the quickly
acquired riches of the corregidor was general. Current opinion
considered these gains as excessive and well above the salary that a
conscientious royal official of high rank might expect. Other members
of colonial society had other reasons for resentment. The higher
clergy was in constant conflict with the corregidores over matters of
patronage or jurisdiction. Typical of the type of conflict was that
which developed between Bishop Moscoso of Cuzco and Corregidor
Arriaga of Tinta. Moscoso wanted some inhabitants of the village of
Yauri arrested, but the corregidor and his teniente opposed such a
measure on the grounds that it was not a matter for ecclesiastical
jurisdiction.[85] The lower clergy, on the other hand, were in very close
and intimate relations with the Indian population. Without any
doubt, they were the social sector of white origin (although many of
them had a considerable admixture of Indian blood) with the greatest
degree of influence over the Indians. They were constantly accused of
using this power exclusively to their own benefit and of systematically
hindering the other whites from entering into any direct contact
with Indians. The fact that so few Indians knew Spanish was considered
their fault; the lower clergy had preferred to learn quechua or aymará,
thus becoming the only Spaniards able to communicate directly with
the Indian community.[86]

The increasing efficiency of the bureaucracy was producing an

[84] 'Relación que hace el Excmo. Sr. Don Manuel de Guirior' in Relaciones de
los Virreyes y Audiencias, p. 41.

[85] Francisco A. Loayza (ed.), La Verdad Desnuda (Lima, 1943), p. 30.

[86] Cf. 'Relación del Estado de los Reinos del Perú que hace . . . el Marqués de
Castel–Fuerte', pp. 42–3.

ever higher degree of tension in the social body. This tension reached
its peak with the visit of Areche. Measures to increase efficiency and
to step up tax collection multiplied: the alcabala (sales tax) was rapidly
raised from 4 to 6 per cent. One of the main preoccupations of the
authorities was to organize the custom houses, where these taxes were
collected, on a firm basis. The introduction of the new plans produced
a chain reaction of upheaval. Let us cite the events connected with the
introduction of these plans at Arequipa in 1780:

'As soon as it was known here (Arequipa) the contents of the orders brought
by Dr. Dn. Juan Bautista Pando to set up the Custom House and be its administrator . . . voices were raised with such virulence that there was fear lest some
fatal event might occur. The orders finally arrived in this city and from January
1st, the day on which the Custom House was opened, things were managed
in a fashion diametrically opposed to the methods employed previously by the
Royal Officials; taxes were levied right and left without exempting even
foodstuffs or goods produced by the Indians by their own work. Pando went
so far as to state publicly that Custom House duties would grow this year
from eighty to more than a hundred and fifty thousand pesos.'[87]

All the upheavals we have mentioned above as occurring in 1780
in various parts of Peru and Upper Peru were triggered by these
attempts to strengthen the central administration.

This does not mean that the whole local society was leagued against
the new incumbents. Conflicts cut so deeply across the whole society,
that this new element was merely added to tensions which already
existed. During the later years of the 1770s, and in the early 1780s, it
became increasingly clear to everybody that the Caroline policy was
not going to be stopped so easily by protest. Some of the upheavals—
as illustrated, for instance, by the case of Arequipa—were successful.
The custom house was dismantled and registration of individuals—
mestizos as well as Indians—for the poll-tax was discontinued. But
even in these cases it was evident that these were short-term victories.
The authorities insistently declared their intention of enforcing their
policies.[88]

The mass of displaced Indians, permanently vagrant and with
such insecure and shifting means of subsistence, was a social sector
easy to mobilize if appropriate leadership and aims were supplied.

[87] 'Relación de lo acaecido en la Ciudad de Arequipa con el Levantamiento de
los Indios e Individuos mal contentos' in Melchor de Paz, op. cit., p. 85.
[88] See for instance letter from Areche to Real Audiencia de la Plata, Lima,
13 June 1780. A.G.I., Audiencia de Charcas, Legajo 595.

We have already described their deviant behaviour. Moreover, given their migratory way of life, they were less under the control of the local curacas or priests. In Pando's account of the events in Arequipa after the establishment of the Custom House, the participation of 'foreign' Indians was conspicuous:

'... in the vicinity of this town (Arequipa), or near it, there is a class of Indians that are called foreigners. . . . The propensity of this caste to drunkenness is undeniable, especially whenever they honour their Patron Saint. . . . The traitors (meaning the leaders of the revolts against the custom house) knew that no others would follow them with more enthusiasm than these miserable drunkards. Thus, having won the support of some of them for the plunder and robbery of the Custom-House, from then on they (the traitors) needed no other incentive on such occasions to find henchmen for their depraved designs.'[89]

VIII

Thus, the course of events may be interpreted as follows: There was permanent resentment among the Indian community against several features of the colonial system. The most conspicuous factors of irritation were the mita and the reparto. Resentment was also caused by the attempts at registration of migrant Indians that had settled on a more or less temporary basis in the vicinity of the already existing villages and towns. Many of the localized Indian riots and upheavals before and after the great uprisings of 1780 may be assigned to these factors. In general, this type of upheaval was geographically limited and of short duration; most of them were based on a few communities with more or less improvised chieftains. They were not very difficult for the local authorities to suppress, and their extension was very limited. Participation in these revolts was not exclusively Indian, but when other groups were involved they were expressing purely local resentments and conflicts. The only previous case which could not be suppressed was the rebellion headed by Juan Santos Atahualpa. But this happened principally because Juan Santos Atahualpa established himself in a frontier region, whence he could out-manoeuvre the Spanish armies and could count on considerable support from tribes living beyond the frontiers of colonial culture. He failed to widen the movement with popular support coming from within Spanish colonial society. The situation developed into a long stalemate in which neither was Juan Santos able to make any progress nor were the government's forces able to vanquish him.

[89] Juan Bautista Pando, 'Diálogo crítico entre el Portero de la Aduana de Arequipa y un Arequipeño' in *Melchor de Paz*, op. cit., p. 137.

With the advent and extension of the Caroline administration, the situation was radically altered. The decisive attempt at modernization it implied carried with it a consequence: conflict was generalized. The reform measures which the administration introduced signified a growing threat to almost every portion of the established network of interests. The whole class structure was affected, from the large merchants and aristocrats in Lima to the lowest poll-tax payers or small-scale Indian traders. Taxes had to be paid, corrupt or inefficient officials might be thrown out, illegal appropriations of land would have to be given back.[90]

The population often reacted to an increase of bureaucratic efficiency with contradictory responses. For instance, many Indians practising trade were protected by laws which decreed that no alcabala (sales tax) was to be collected from them, provided the goods they traded in were produced directly by them. When the custom house was established as a separate branch of the administration, many Indian traders were forced to pay alcabalas for the first time; either because it was patently clear that they were trading in goods produced by others or else because custom officials tried to raise the tax in whatever form it could be done. This naturally produced resentment on their part. On the other hand, they could expect more protection from a more law-abiding bureaucracy in their claims concerning the usurpation of Indian land.

The arrival of Visitor-General Areche in Peru (14 June 1777) gave this modernizing trend a decisive acceleration. Areche's strong hand was immediately felt and resented. One must not forget that the Crown urged him to increase revenues badly needed for the war with England. But the possibility of raising these revenues was dependent on the fact that there was already in existence a bureaucracy which was needed to carry out orders.

Many threatened groups joined forces to try to withstand these innovations. Artisans, traders, threatened members of the old bureaucracy, corregidores, land usurpers, were all under fire at the same time, and they reacted correspondingly against the newcomers and their impositions. All the disturbances which we have examined in the first months of 1780 in Arequipa, Huancavélica, Cuzco, and other places, were motivated by this reaction. For instance, in Cuzco the revolt of Lorenzo Farfán de los Godos included members of

---

[90] Letter from Mata Linares to Escobedo, N.7, Cuzco, 14 March 1785. *A.G.I.*, Audiencia Cuzco, Legajo 35. Mata Linares considered that the fact of checking illegal appropriations of land was the major cause for the rebellions.

the old administration and also silversmiths. The former were presumably threatened with losing their jobs, the latter with paying more taxes.

Faced with such sustained pressures from the central government, the local dominant classes had no other recourse but to try to mobilize the lower sectors of the population; this was done in many of the disturbances which broke out in 1780. As it was progressively clear that the activities of the new bureaucrats were not going to be stopped easily, more and more elements of the higher and middle classes were ready to support the demands of the Indians, although these demands were not necessarily expressed always as grievances against tax collectors. As a sizeable proportion of Indians practised some form of trade, protest was often directed against custom house officials. But given the fact that an increased degree of violence of any origin could be expected to dampen the resolution with which the bureaucracy was prepared to enforce its orders, and could even stop them altogether, other factors of Indian irritation received support from dominant sectors of the society. Consequently, by the middle of the year 1780 there were constant rumours of mass movements, rumours which were spread by every party interested in changing whatever conditions they might deem undesirable. There was a background murmur of popular discontent which all the groups with grievances tried to link up with their own demands. Corregidores maintained that this discontent was consequence of the priests' exploitation of their own communities; bureaucrats accused both priests and corregidores of similar misdeeds. For instance, in Chayanta, Tomas Catari, supported by the priest Merlos, had a prolonged conflict with Corregidor Alos over his right to be appointed cacique, and he too looked for popular backing for his demands.

Against such a convulsive background, José Gabriel Tupan Amarú started his revolt on 4 November 1780, in the province of Tinta. It is important to bear in mind that at this time an intense conflict was taking place between the corregidor of Tinta, Arriaga, and the bishop of Cuzco, Moscoso. This conflict opened the door for a coalition (of which there are several other examples) in which violence served at the same time to eliminate an enemy and contributed to weaken the resoluteness of the bureaucratic arm. Enough evidence has been offered of the involvement of sectors of the upper classes of Cuzco in the outbreak of the uprising of Tupac Amarú. Not only Bishop Moscoso, but also others like the Ugarte brothers, distinguished members of the Cabildo, are prominent cases in point. That José

Gabriel Tupac Amarú was expecting support from powerful groups of Cuzco is quite apparent in contemporary documents.[91]

But, in order to succeed, Tupac Amarú had to mobilize the masses. For such an attempt, apart from charismatic leadership, a clear-cut enemy was needed for the Indians. For the reasons we have already indicated, the corregidor was such an enemy. Thus, his first act was to imprison Arriaga, corregidor of the province of Tinta. This was done on 4 November. After a trial, Arriaga was executed on 10 November under charges of abuse and misbehaviour. Tupac claimed to have direct orders for such an action from the king of Spain himself, Charles III.

The procedure adopted for the execution of Arriaga was calculated to fulfil the requisites of charismatic leadership. The execution was performed with due pomp and circumstance. In the central square of Tungasuca, José Gabriel Tupac Amarú hanged the corregidor, surrounding the gallows with a troop of armed men, Indians as well as whites. All the formalities expected from a man in a position of power were observed. Combining his claims of being of Inca royal descent with the pretence of acting on orders from the king of Spain, Tupac Amarú produced an impressive image of power and authority. For the lower-class Indian, especially for the unattached, who through his migratory habits had no strong dependence on local chieftains, he had every claim to be taken as the ruler.

There is another important component in the image of authority given by Tupac Amarú. For the class of migratory Indians, to support him meant to become a member of a movement endowed with power and strength. The constitution of such a type of social coalition which seemed strong enough to put an end to so much injustice and suffering fostered the propensity to violence of the individuals participating in it.[92] But at the same time, the mass movement became too

[91] Cf. Loayza (ed.), *La Verdad Desnuda*.

[92] This feature of social coalitions is formally elaborated in O. Cornblit, 'Conflicto, cooperación y cambio: interpretación formal de un modelo de cambio social para América Latina', *Centro de Investigaciones Sociales, Instituto Torcuato Di Tella* (Buenos Aires, 1967), p. 37. Some sociological categories may also be connected with it. For instance, 'relative deprivation', which refers to a population which suddenly feels that 'what was an impossible aspiration in the past is such no longer'. In situations of this kind, a quick shift from apathy to revolutionary action is to be expected. See Lewis A. Coser, 'Violence and Social Structure', in Jules H. Massermann (ed.), *Violence and War* (New York and London: Grunne and Stratton, 1963), p. 37. Also 'anomy' is a suitable category. This last term has unfortunately been given so many meanings that it needs careful qualification.

powerful for those members of the middle or higher classes, who up to that moment had been ready to be its potential allies. Thus, the same sectors which had induced and supported Indian riots and which did not hesitate to mobilize them on behalf of their own interests, became immediately threatened by the intensity and violence of the mobilization, which in a short time got out of hand.

This is why Tupac Amarú, who was expecting support from certain important sectors in Cuzco, received none. The very fact of his receiving such splendid mass support cut him off from the possibility of building a successful coalition with those urban groups which had shown themselves prepared for a joint revolt against the evils produced by the central administration. Thus, the main support for Tupac Amarú came from his own community, where he was a conspicuous leader and from the mass foreign Indians who were roaming about or had recently settled in or nearby his region of influence. Significantly enough, rebellions spread like wildfire throughout those regions where the proportion of foreign Indians was highest: that is, La Paz, Chuquisaca, and the provinces of the bishopric of Cuzco lying towards Lake Titicaca. It was easily checked in regions north of Cuzco in central and northern Peru, where the proportion of foreign Indians was much lower. This does not mean that only foreign Indians were involved in the upheavals. There were enough local grievances among Indians to drive a part of the original Indians to the side of the rebels. To this we must add the high geographical mobility of the 'foreign' Indians, which was a substantial factor in the rapid spread of the revolt.

It is also significant that the majority of the Indians 'aristocracy' fought against the rebels, as, for instance, the Indians leaders Pumacahua and Choqueguanca. They accused Tupac Amarú of being an usurper and a bastard and maintained that his claims of royal descent were ill-founded. They were of decisive importance for the defeat of the rebellion. The twelve royal ayllus of Cuzco also opposed the rebels and contributed armed forces to the defence of the city.[93] In addition, a high proportion of caciques remained loyal to the Spanish authorities, notwithstanding the fact that under the pressure of the

What S. de Grazia calls 'acute anomia', a psychological condition arising out of lack of leadership, could also be appropriate for the case of the migratory Indians. See Sebastian De Grazia, The Political Community: a study of Anomia (University of Chicago Press, 3rd impression, 1966), pp. 110 ff.

[93] Letter from Mata Linares to Galvez, Cuzco, 19 March 1786. A.G.I., Audiencia Audiencia Cuzco, Legajo 35.

mobilized Indians many changed back and forth in the course of the struggles. This shows how well these chieftains were integrated into the colonial system, favouring the *status quo* when the threat against it was too strong. But the conflicts within the Indian colonial society led at the same time to the emergence of new rebel leaders, who proved powerful when carried on the crest of the revolutionary wave.

In some cases, the alliance between the threatened local higher classes and the lower dispossessed and displaced Indians lasted much longer than in Cuzco. From this point of view, one of the most interesting foci of revolt was Oruro, where a significant proportion of the higher classes were leaders in the revolt against the authorities. That mine-owners like the Rodriguez family and others with them were prepared to go so far in such a dangerous alliance, is to be accounted for not only the fact that they were facing a tax threat from the bureaucrats, they were also in very difficult financial straits and needed the support of the lower classes to get rid of their creditors, as in fact they did during the first period of their revolt. They had no option but to join forces with the lower classes and support the violence through which this coalition expressed itself. The very fragility of their economic position offered them no other alternative. That the risk was very great was proved by the fact that they were only able to escape with considerable difficulty the growing pressure of popular demands; there was a time when they were almost submerged by the mass revolt. Then, only by cutting their allegiance to the lower classes and building a new alliance with the local curacas, could they oppose the mobilized mass. Thus, eliminating in a first step their upper-class enemies and regaining control of the situation in a second step, they completed successfully the goals of their movement.

One might say in conclusion that the Oruro-type rebellion was the one sought by other local higher groups in other regions. But the overwhelming speed and violence with which the lower layers of society mobilized themselves into the uprising, in most places prevented the continuation of the primitive alliance and drove their would-be allies over to the enemy camp.

AGRARIAN EXPANSION AND INDUSTRIAL DEVELOPMENT IN ARGENTINA, 1880–1930*

by Ezequiel Gallo

THE HISTORICAL period I propose to analyse in this paper was marked by a great expansion of the Argentine economy and society as a whole, an expansion which, by the 1920s, had gone on for more than forty years. Few of the authors who have studied the period would argue with this statement. Yet much of the work they have handed down to us fails to take this extremely important fact sufficiently into consideration.

They tend to concentrate on what we might call 'the negative aspects of the process' rather than on the expansion itself. The reasons for this are easy enough to understand: the majority of these studies were mainly concerned with the analysis of the Argentinian economy's less successful performance in the more recent past. Thus the authors were particularly interested in the aspects which were to have a negative effect on the subsequent development of the economy: the consolidation of large-scale landownership in the Pampas region and the lack of an energetic policy of industrial development.

It is not the intention of this paper at this point to challenge the validity of this attitude; indeed, we are indebted to many of these studies for the most satisfactory analysis available of this particular set of historical circumstances. Nevertheless, certain important distortions may be attributed to this attitude among recent economists and economic historians. The risk of distortion becomes even greater, when it comes to analysing the behaviour of the various social groups

* A longer version of this paper was read in the course of the Seminar organized by the Latin American Centre of St. Antony's College, Oxford, on the subject of 'Economic Development in Argentina', directed by Professors R. Carr and H. J. Habakkuk and Dr. K. Griffin. Their comments, as well as those made by others attending the seminar, were very useful to me in preparing this shortened version. I would like to express my special thanks to Professor Carr and to the Argentinian economists O. Braun, L. Geller, and J. Katz.

involved on the basis of the premisses established by such economic (or sociological) models. Just as the variables to which the greatest importance is attached may not always have been the most significant in a given historical context, so the actions of the participants in a situation are frequently judged in relation to marginal events or, what is worse, in the light of events that have occurred outside the framework of their own experience.

In the following paper I shall discuss some of the conclusions that emerge from some recent studies of the various social groups linked to the process of industrialization during the period under consideration. It seems to me that these conclusions are indicative of the kind of attitude I have described.

I. Recent works on the subject

Guido di Tella and Manuel Zymelman,[1] in the most comprehensive version yet available of our economic history, have pointed out that a change of direction in the economy became necessary around 1914. The forces which had until that time determined the growth rate of the economy were beginning to show signs of flagging, and in particular the ready availability of virgin lands in the border areas of the Pampas was a thing of the past. As a result, attention was beginning to be diverted towards the comparatively more advantageous industrial sector. Since these symptoms did not, however, suffice to modify the relative importance of agriculture as against that of industry as much as might have been expected, the authors have chosen to call the period from 1914 to 1932 the 'Great Delay'.

Similar conclusions, though based on methodologically different premises, were previously reached by Aldo Ferrer,[2] who is also of the opinion that Argentina did not give sufficient impulse to industrialization at a time when changed circumstances demanded it.

These assumptions raise a number of questions relating to the obstacles standing in the way of change. Some of the replies to these questions put the blame on the behaviour of the various social groups involved in the process. Two approaches in particular will be considered.

The first interpretation is focused on the social groups that impeded the development of manufacturing industries. The principal culprits

[1] Guido di Tella y Manuel Zymelman, Las Etapas del Desarrollo Económico Argentino (Editorial Universitaria de Buenos Aires, Buenos Aires, 1967).

[2] Aldo Ferrer, La Economía Argentina. Las Etapas de su Desarrollo y Problemas Actuales (Fondo de Cultura Económica, Mexico–Buenos Aires, 1963).

are held to be the great landowners whose control of political and economic power was at the time unchallenged. The authors mentioned above subscribe, with variations of emphasis, to this view.[3]

The second interpretation maintains that insufficient pressure was brought to bear by those social sectors with a direct interest in the expansion of the manufacturing industries. Roberto Cortes Conde[4] has indicated some of the conditions adverse to the emergence of a solid and independent body of industrialists. These were (i) that the most important industries were closely linked to the agrarian sector (refrigeration, flour mills, etc.), which was bound to limit their independence; (ii) that in the other branches of industry there was a predominance of small establishments, some of them even craft industries, which limited their strength; (iii) the exceedingly large proportion of foreign nationals among industrialists, who remained remote from politics, since immigrants did not generally participate actively in public life.

Dependence, weakness and isolation were therefore at the root of the industrialists' lack of influence on the elaboration of official economic policy. The subject of political isolation has been taken up by Oscar Cornblit[5] in his recent study of the relationship between the indigenous political institutions and the immigrants; he suggests that the institutional weakness of the industrialists was a result of their failure to communicate sufficiently with the local political parties. Cornblit draws our attention particularly to the example of the Radical Party, which was in power from 1916 to 1930. In this particular case, Cornblit explains the isolation of the industrialists by the anti-foreign attitude of the Radical leadership, which deprived them of a solid political platform from which they might have brought pressure to bear upon government circles.

In the following pages we shall comment briefly on some aspects of these two hypotheses.[6] Our own analysis, however, should be

[3] Ferrer seems to consider that the great landowners were 'obstacles' at all times. During the period of rapid economic expansion, the favourable international trade situation and the ready availability of fertile land are held to have made these characteristics imperceptible for a time; thus the country is held to have grown and developed 'in spite' of this group. Ibid., p. 115.

[4] Roberto Cortés Conde, 'Problemas del Crecimiento Industrial' (1870–1914) in Torcuato di Tella, Gino Germani, Jorge Graciarena y colaboradores, *Argentina Sociedad de Masas* (Editorial Universitaria de Buenos Aires, Buenos Aires, 1965).

[5] Oscar Cornblit, 'Inmigrantes y Empresarios en la Política Argentina', in *Desarrollo Económico*, Vol. VI, No. 24 (January–March 1967, Buenos Aires).

[6] The works commented on in this paper have been chosen because they are

applied only to the industrial sector as a whole. At present, the material available does not form an extension of the conclusions of this paper to individual industries.

II. *Agrarian expansion and the development of manufacturing industries*

Both hypotheses take for granted a relationship of conflict between the agrarian sector and the industrial sector. Indeed, for some authors this conflict constituted in itself the most serious obstacle in the way of a 'satisfactory' industrial expansion. And it was in tariff policy that this relationship of conflict reached its climax.

However, a closer look at the information at our disposal throws serious doubts on the validity of this assumption. Doubt becomes acute when we confront the assumption with two kinds of historical evidence:

(a) It is a commonplace to say that by 1920 Argentina was still far from being a fully industrialized country. None the less, after the agrarian expansion got under way in 1880, industry too progressed considerably; what is more, at certain stages the development of industry advanced at a spectacular rate. Although the statistics leave much to be desired, it is possible to deduce from the existing figures a high rate of industrial development in the period between the census of 1895 and that of 1914.

TABLE I

Industrial growth (1895–1914)

	No. of establishments	No. of employees	Capital ($)
1895	22,204	174,782	327,397,366
1914	48,779	410,201	1,787,662,295

Source: *Segundo Censo Nacional* (1895), Vol. III, and *Tercer Censo Nacional* (1914), Vol. VII.

Our conclusion appears to be confirmed by a comparison between these figures and the production figures of industry published by the C.E.P.A.L.

---

the most serious and sophisticated versions of convictions deeply rooted in scholarly writings and essays on the subject. Moreover, our comments merely have a bearing on certain aspects of these works, which in many other respects have contributed much to our understanding of the historical reality. Finally, the critical comments which follow are also relevant to much of my own work. In the past, I have been an enthusiastic supporter of the hypothesis I now criticize, and have defended it in previous works, generally with less rigour than the authors mentioned here, though with the same, if not greater, orthodoxy. See e.g. 'Industrialisation in Argentina' (in collaboration with Jorge Katz) in Claudio Veliz (ed.) *Handbook of Latin America* (Anthony Blond, London, 1967).

TABLE II

Volume of industrial production

(Basic Index 1950 = 100)

1900	9·2	1915	18·2
1901	9·2	1916	18·7
1902	9·8	1917	18·5
1903	10·8	1918	22·1
1904	11·8	1919	23·0
1905	13·8	1920	23·8
1906	14·5	1921	25·1
1907	16·1	1922	27·9
1908	17·1	1923	32·6
1909	16·9	1924	34·4
1910	20·7	1925	37·3
1911	22·2	1926	36·6
1912	21·0	1927	38·9
1913	22·3	1928	43·4
1914	20·3	1929	45·6
		1930	45·1

Source: C.E.P.A.L.: 'El Desarrollo Económico de la Argentina', Vol. IV
(mimeographed), Santiago de
Chile, 1960.

At the same time, the census of 1914 shows the progress made by the
country in the field of import substitution; in the field of consumer
goods, especially foodstuffs, substitution had gone a long way (see
Table III). Taken together, these figures enable us to establish that the
first ten years of the twentieth century (particularly the years 1907–13)
saw a rapid growth of the industrial sector. For periods prior to the
census of 1895, the available information is even more fragmented and
scanty. None the less, from the rather impressionistic material we have
at our disposal it would seem that the first great spurt of the manufacturing industries took place during the 1880s. At this time we see
the establishment of the first modern plants in food industries, with refrigeration and flour mills in the forefront.[7] As a result of the crisis of 1890
and the corresponding reduction in imports, a large number of factories
were built in the vicinity of Buenos Aires.[8] Thus the census of 1895

[7] Adolfo Dorfman, *Evolución Industrial Argentina* (Editorial Losada, Buenos
Aires, 1942), p. 268 ff. See also the extremely interesting report by Worthington,
special envoy sent by the British Government to study the industrial problem in
Argentina. *Parliamentary Papers*, Vol. XCVI, Session 1–7 February to 9 August
1899, and 2–17 October to 27 October 1899.

D

showed a high degree of growth and the creation of new industries fomented, firstly, by the great expansion of agricultural exports and, secondly, by the import restrictions imposed by the events of 1890. The extremely detailed report compiled in 1899 by a British special envoy gives the impression that the most modern as well as the largest industrial plants were those which had sprung up in the 1880s, while those which had been founded in the years following the crisis of 1890 were, on the contrary, in an extremely precarious position; the reason for this decline the report found in the fall of the price of gold.[9]

It does not, therefore, seem rash to suggest that until 1914 the rise of industry coincided, in general terms, with the great export booms. The fairly widely held belief that the First World War had a particularly

TABLE III

Type of industry	Production (1)	Imports yearly average (1911–15) (1)	Consumption	Percentage covered by domestic industry
Food	1,004·7	102·6	1,107·1	90·7
Clothing and Cosmetics	160·3	21·9	182·3	87·9
Building	229·6	57·9	287·5	79·9
Furniture, Cars, etc.	87·1	37·1	124·1	70·2
Objets d'Art and Ornaments	16·1	9·5	25·6	63·0
Household utensils, etc.	94·3	189·3	283·6	33·2
Chemicals	56·3	90·1	146·3	37·9
Graphic arts	39·7	6·2	45·9	86·4
Textiles	40·2	138·1	178·4	22·6
Various	147·7	101·8	249·5	59·1
TOTAL	1,875·8	754·5	2,630·3	71·3

Source: *Tercer Censo Nacional*, Vol. VIII, p. 448.
(1) In millions of dollars m/n.

[8] Ibid. Also M. G. and E. T. Mulhall, *Handbook of the River Plate* (Buenos Aires and London, 1892), p. 293. For an earlier period, see Emilio Daireaux, *Vida y Costumbres en el Plata*, Vol. II, 'Industrias y Productos' (Buenos Aires, 1888), p. 118 ff.
[9] *Parliamentary Papers*, Vol. XCVI (1899): report by T. Worthington, 'Trade in certain South American countries.'

stimulating effect on industry (because of the natural slackening of
competition from abroad) seems to be contradicted by the annual
figures given by C.E.P.A.L. (see Table II), which show a marked
decline of the growth rate throughout the war.[10] A marked recovery
occurs in the 1920s and particularly during the five years from 1925 to
1929, which happen to coincide with the last great boom experienced
by the export sector.

The correlation between a rise in exports and industrial development
was certainly not peculiar to Argentina. A vast volume of literature
has described similar instances in other countries. The conclusions
reached are relevant to our purpose, in that they refer to areas with
which the Argentina of that time is commonly compared (Australia,
Canada, the west of the United States, etc.). Watkins[11] provides us
with a summary of the model put forward by most of the literature
on the subject:

'The fundamental assumption of the *staple theory* is that staple exports are the
leading sector of the economy and set the pace for economic growth. The
limited—at first possibly non-existant—domestic market, and the factor
proportion—an abundance of land relative to labour and capital—create a
comparative advantage in resource-intensive exports or staples. Economic
development will be a process of diversification around an export base.'

[10] Di Tella and Zymelman accept these conclusions but maintain, on the basis
of a survey by Bunge, that the positive aspect of the war years was the fact that
they gave rise to a significant degree of industrial concentration (pp. 306 ff.). The
figures put forward by C.E.P.A.L. show, moreover, that the textile and dairy
industries performed well. But these conclusions do not modify our point of
view significantly, since we are interested in the over-all performance of the
industrial sector. It may be worth while pointing out that the process of industrial
concentration in certain food-producing branches had progressed considerably in
the years preceding the outbreak of the war. See Ernesto Tornquist, *El Desarrollo
Económico de la Argentina en los Ultimos Cincuenta Años* (Buenos Aires, 1920),
chapters III and IV.

[11] Melville Watkins, 'A Staple Theory of Economic Growth', *The Canadian
Journal of Economics and Political Science*, Vol. XXIX, No. 2 (May 1963). See also
Richard Caves, 'Vent for surplus models of trade and development' in Baldwin,
Trade, Growth and the Balance of Payments, Essays in honour of G. Haberler (North
Holland Publishing House, Amsterdam, 1965) and Douglas North, 'Location
Theory and Regional Economic Growth', *Journal of Political Economy*, LXIII
(June 1955). The analysis of the development of the 'open spaces' made by di
Tella and Zymelman (chapter VI) is not altogether different from that contained
in the above-mentioned works. The problem is that the socio-political variables
of the model of stages elaborated by Rostow cannot be applied to the situations
set out in the 'staple theory'.

Given the special conditions of the international market at the time under consideration, the continuity of the process of economic growth depended on the capacity of the new regions to continue producing at lower cost than the old agricultural areas. The new countries fulfilled this condition in various ways, either by resorting to new staples (e.g. Canada), or to additional stretches of virgin land (e.g. Argentina), or else by introducing economies of scale and technological innovations in the various sectors of production.[12] The possibility of adopting one or several of these courses enabled these countries or regions to enjoy a long period of continuous economic expansion. However, it should not necessarily be inferred that a continuous expansion of exports is bound to have favourable repercussions on the process of growth in other sectors of the economy (unless these are directly linked to the export sector, as in the case of transport). In its analysis of the relationship between the export sector and the rest of the economy, the literature of the staple theory has stressed the importance of the part played by the technology of the various staples:

'The technology of the staple determines economic structure in two ways, firstly by backward and forward linkages with local industry that supply products or services to it or that purchase its own product for further processing, and secondly by the distribution of income by the staple industry.'[13]

Baldwin was the first to illustrate this relationship by comparing an area of plantations with one that was primarily wheat-producing. Both the backward and the forward linkage effects of wheat, as well as the widely distributed income obtained from it, favoured the establishment of industries in the wheat-growing area.[14]

[12] Though the availability of virgin lands constituted the greatest dynamic stimulant, it should not be deduced from this that there were no other equally important elements. The institutional reforms realized in the 1880s, the technological innovations introduced into agrarian exploitation and the rationalization of the trading systems were significant factors also. See Roberto Cortés Conde and Ezequiel Gallo (h), *La Formación de la Argentina Contemporánea* (ed. Paidós, Buenos Aires, 1967), *passim*.

[13] J. W. McCarthy: 'The Staple Approach in Australian Economic History' in *Business Archives and History* (The University of Sydney, Vol. IV, No. 1, February 1964).

[14] Regarding the wheat production function: 'First, a family-size farm gives an efficient scale of production. In particular, large scale production based on the intensive use of cheap, imported labour is not the best form of economic organization. Furthermore, the absolute amount of capital required is less for the optimum

North[15] exemplified this phenomenon in his comparative study of the development of the west and the south of the United States, and similar conclusions have been drawn for Canada and Australia.[16]

Given these characteristics, the strategic variable in the process of industrialization undergone by these regions has been the steady expansion of demand, which in turn resulted from the increase in incomes generated by the successful performance of the export sector. And Argentina does not seem to have been an exception to this rule, though the consequent industrial development was less spectacular than that attained in Australia and Canada. But possibly this relative backwardness was due to less dramatic (or more prosaic) causes than has generally been supposed (sociological, cultural, or political). One such cause must be, for example, the absence of coal and iron, which Argentina lacked and which were vital, in the nineteenth century, to all industrial development.[17]

(b) Many other factors intervened in the process of development of the new countries, and of these protective tariff barriers were not the least significant; but here again it seems that the situation in which Argentinian industry found itself has been much exaggerated. During the first period (1870–1914), protectionist laws for industry proliferated: in 1876, 1883, 1887, 1891, and 1905. The recent study of this subject

---

size of a production unit, and the level of managerial and technical skill need not be so high for a productive unit of the most efficient size'. Obviously, the comparison is with areas of plantation economy. Robert Baldwin: 'Agriculture in Newly Settled Regions', in Carl K. Eicher and others, *Agriculture in Economic Development* (McGraw Hill, U.S.A., 1964).

[15] Douglas North, *The Economic Growth of the United States. 1790–1860* (Norton, New York, 1966).

[16] For Australia, the article by McCarthy already quoted. For Canada, among others, Gordon W. Bertran, 'Economic Growth in Canadian Industry. The Staple Theory and the Take Off Hypothesis', in *The Canadian Journal of Economics and Political Science*, Vol. XXIX, No. 2 (May 1963).

[17] Recently, for example, Cole and Deane have explained the halting way in which Argentinian industry developed by pointing out that the vast majority of immigrants came from the European south (Italy and Spain), where the socio-cultural context had not been of a kind to foster an aptitude for industrial activities. Oddly enough, there is no mention of the absence of coal and iron ore, though a lack of these raw materials is brought forward as part of the explanation when it comes to analysing the industrial process in other countries (e.g. Scandinavia). See W. A. Cole and Phyllis Deane: 'The Growth of National Incomes', pp. 27–8 and 38–9, in M. M. Postan and H. J. Habakkuk (eds.), *The Cambridge Economic History of Europe*, Vol. VI, 'The Industrial Revolution and After', Part 1 (Cambridge, 1965).

by Díaz Alejandro[18] certainly does not reinforce the desolate picture of 'disprotection', to which a certain kind of literature had accustomed us. The author maintains that, by 1913, the tariff level of Argentina compared favourably with those of Canada and Australia and was slightly lower than that of the United States.

More relevant to our argument is the fact that the greater part of public opinion tended to feel that the level of tariffs was excessive. This is shown by the work of Ricardo Pillado and the exhortations of the Socialist Party. The Radical Party was first split in 1909 because the group led by Pedro Molina maintained that the party did not oppose the advances of protectionist legislation firmly enough. In 1911, 72 per cent of those who replied to a questionnaire carried out by the *Revista Argentina de Ciencias Políticas* replied in favour of a total free trade policy.[19] This opinion was shared by foreign observers like Watson and Worthington[20] who had studied the situation of Argentinian industry. As has been suggested by almost all the authors who have treated the subject, tariffs were tending to stabilize from 1913 onward, though this did not impede the great industrial recovery that occurred during the 1920s. Later we shall come back to the subject of tariff policy after the end of World War I.

If one accepts the evidence put forward here, the analysis of the various groups concerned in the process of industrialization must be based on assumptions different from those that have been accepted in the past. In the first place, at least until 1914, the economic and institutional system was sufficiently flexible for a highly satisfactory industrial expansion to take place. At the same time, the obstacles in the way of expansion, as the case of the tariff barriers shows, were far from insurmountable. Secondly, as has been pointed out repeatedly, the majority of industrialists in 1914 (66 per cent) were European immigrants who had recently arrived in Argentina. The spectacular

[18] Carlos F. Díaz Alejandro, 'The Argentine Tariff, 1906–1940', in *Oxford Economic Papers*, Vol. XIX, No. 1 (March 1967). A more concise statistical analysis of the evolution of tariffs has been carried out by Vicente Vazquez Presedo as part of his Ph.D. thesis at the University of Oxford ('The role of foreign trade and migration in the development of the Argentine economy. 1870–1914'). His conclusions give support to the point of view expressed in the text.

[19] Darío Cantón: 'La primera encuesta política argentina', *Documento de Trabajo No. 38 del Centro de Investigaciones Sociales del Instituto Torcuato di Tella* (Buenos Aires, 1967, mimeographed).

[20] N. L. Watson, *Argentina as a Market* (London, 1908), chapters III and IV. In the opinion of this author, the most serious problem the industrialists had to face was that of the trade unions (p. 41 ff.).

economic expansion of 1880-1914 had given rise to a process of great social mobility among the new arrivals, a large proportion of whom had rapidly ascended in social status. This process of great intra-generational social mobility has recently been assessed by Gino Germani. His conclusions for the period 1870-1914 were as follows:

'As can be seen, as a result of the expansion of the middle classes, two thirds of these were bound to be composed of people with lower class origins, and in the case of the foreigners—where it was no longer a matter of intergenerational mobility but of intragenerational mobility—it was the immigrants themselves, workers, journeymen and peasants, who transformed themselves into shopkeepers, clerks, etc. In the foreign sector the middle classes consisted mainly of self made men.'[21]

In fact, the economic, institutional, and social picture that has been outlined does not lead us to suppose that there was a relationship of acute conflict between the agrarian export sector and the industrial groups. This becomes even more obvious when we consider that the expansion of industry depended to a great extent on the successful performance of the rural sector.[22] To this we may add other examples of ways in which the interests of both groups coincided. Among them, the foreign exchange policy and the course of action to be followed with regard to the ever more aggressive trade unions were perhaps the most important.[23]

If these observations are valid, concepts like those mentioned previously (obstacles, weakness, etc.) become relative. A correct approach to the subject would oblige us to pose the questions differently. That is to say: What prevented the tariff barriers from being *higher*? Or, which industries suffered particularly from a lack of protection?[24]

[21] Gino Germani, 'La Movilidad Social en la Argentina', in Lipset and Bendix, *La Movilidad Social en la Sociedad Industrial* (EUDEBA, Buenos Aires, 1963).

[22] Nothing seems to have been published on the relationship between landowners and industrialists, apart from a monograph written by H. Berlatzky and S. Novick of the Department of Sociology, University of Buenos Aires, based mainly on the information contained in the Bulletins of the Unión Industrial. They tend to decry the idea of any conflict between the two groups.

[23] On the subject of the price of gold and the activities of the trade unions, see the works of Worthington and Watson, respectively, and Américo Guerrero *La Industria Argentina. Su Orígen, Organización y Desarrollo* (Buenos Aires, 1944), for the constant attempts made by industrialists to find satisfactory solutions.

[24] A balanced study of this problem would require us to identify the industries that were 'overprotected'. See, e.g. for the industry manufacturing sacks for exported wheat, James Scobie, *Revolution on the Pampas. A Social History of Argentine Wheat, 1960-1910* (University of Texas, 1964, pp. 95-6 and 131. For

For the reasons mentioned above I shall not attempt to discuss the second of the questions posed. Regarding both of them, however, it is possible that some of the suggestions contained in the works of Cornblit and Cortes Conde, particularly those referring to isolation, may still be relevant. The same could be said regarding dependence, though in this case it would be necessary to specify the concept more clearly. Dependence on the agrarian sector means more than the fact that industries like the flour mills or refrigeration plants were predominant in the industrial sector of the economy. To the extent that, as we have seen, every kind of industry was influenced by the performance of the agrarian sector, all industries were, to use the word, 'dependent'. Indeed, it would not be rash to maintain that the tensions between the first group of industries and the rural landowners were at certain times more acute than those existing between the landowners and the rest of industry. The well-known example of the refrigeration industry in the 1920s is a clear illustration of this.[25]

The need to keep the agrarian sector competitive was no doubt the main argument against a frankly protectionist policy. Higher tariff barriers might of course well have made it less competitive by raising the price of production or by inviting the countries buying agrarian products to take reprisals against Argentina. There is no reason to suppose that the industrialists were indifferent to considerations of this kind.

III. *The complexity of the agrarian export sector*

The problem under consideration becomes rather more complicated when we look at it from another angle. One of the hypotheses listed at the beginning of this article concerns the rigid opposition of the great landowners. In this respect, too, the information available puts the assumption in doubt. As can be seen from the brief description of the tariff situations, the relative stability of tariff levels in the customs policy did not make itself felt until the years 1913–25. This point of view is accepted by several of the authors who have written on the subject.[26]

---

sugar, see Ricardo Pillado, *Política Comercial Argentina. Contribución a su estudio* (Buenos Aires, 1906).

[25] The thesis of Peter Smith (University of Columbia) deals exhaustively with the conflict between the refrigeration industry and the cattle ranchers in the 1920s.

[26] Díaz Alejandro, Di Tella y Zymelman and Cornblit share this point of view. The Chairman of the *Unión Industrial*, Luis Colombo, has also maintained that after 1913 the tariff had become stationary when it had not actually gone down. See his *Levántate y Anda* (Buenos Aires, 1930), p. 123 ff.

In this connection, it is important to realize that from 1916 until 1930, political power passed to the party generally identified with 'the rising middle classes'. The 'growing rigidity' of the tariff policy thus coincided with the time when political power was slipping out of the hands of the traditional ruling classes. And what is more, it was precisely the representatives in congress of the new popular parties, radicals and socialists, who opposed most actively any attempt to raise tariff barriers.[27]

The attitude of both these groups is less surprising if one considers each in its historical context.

The Socialist party elaborated its programme in the years from 1896 to 1914; it acted within the framework established by the European Social Democrats, though it was influenced by the Socialist parties of Australia and New Zealand. The writings of Juan B. Justo, unchallenged leader of the Argentinian Socialists at this time, contain all the ideas on which the political platform of Argentinian Socialism was based.[28]

From the very beginning of its existence, the party based its programme on the assumption that Argentina was experiencing an important process of economic and social expansion which, while being anchored in a rapid development of the rural sector, implied a significant development of the manufacturing industries.[29]

On the basis of this assumption, the Socialist party concentrated its political action mainly on the defence and improvement of the standard of living of the industrial working class. In the pursuit of this objective, the Socialist party resolutely opposed two kinds of measures: legislation tending towards a devaluation of the Argentinian peso and any attempt to raise the tariff barriers. Both measures would have had an adverse effect on the standard of living of the workers

[27] See O. Cornblit, op. cit., and Diaz Alejandro, op. cit.

[28] See specially the following: Estudios sobre la Moneda (Buenos Aires, 1912), and Internacionalismo y Patria (Buenos Aires, 1933).

[29] In the first issue of La Vanguardia (7 April 1894), Justo wrote as follows: 'This country is becoming transformed. The open and undivided plains . . . which were common property, have been succeeded by enclosed fields, soon to cover the entire surface of arable land. Large scale agriculture developed where twenty years ago farmers had cultivated a few smallholdings. The railway has killed off the carts. The large ports have to a great extent made the tramp steamers obsolete. The Central Fruit Market has taken the place of the old stalls. And industry, though it is in a rudimentary state, has undergone the same modifications. In Buenos Aires the shoe and hat factories, the large metal works and furniture factories, have largely done away with the samll workshops; in Tucumán the old presses are replaced by vast sugar-mills, while in Santa Fé the flour mills proliferate where before there had not even been any ovens'.

(in the case of the tariffs, it must be remembered that despite import substitution, a significant proportion of the consumer goods purchased by the workers was still imported). Justo gave clear expression to the socialist attitude towards the problem of tariffs:

'By this we mean . . . that we are in favour of free competition between nations, that we firmly approve and support the principle of free trade and repudiate utterly the archaic doctrine which some have tried to resuscitate in the last few decades and which pretends to protect the nation's labour by surrounding it with customs barriers.'[30]

The socialists were not alone in opposing protectionism. Throughout the period under consideration, the anarchist trade unions pronounced themselves repeatedly in favour of free trade.[31] This attitude on the part of the working-class parties and the trade unions has been criticized *in retrospect* by certain authors, who compared it to that of the Australian Labour Party which in 1906 supported a substantial increase in tariffs. What has not been pointed out in this connection is the fact that by that time there was a considerable difference between the Argentinian and the Australian economies: while in Argentina the jobs available had multiplied tremendously, in Australia a decade of unemployment had gone before the legislation of 1906.[32]

As has been pointed out, tariffs showed a tendency to stagnate during the years of Radical government (1916–30). In his message to the nation in 1920, President Irigoyen explained the executive's point of view as follows:

'Our tariff protection should be limited to those industries which are capable of promoting the general welfare of the country and of cheapening articles of general consumption, and should not be such as to render difficult the importation of foreign merchandise.

'Subject to this rational consideration, the foreign product ought not to inspire mistrust, and the task of the government should consist in endeavouring to secure that the national article does not exceed it in price, and should improve on it in quality if possible.'[33]

---

[30] Juan B. Justo, *Internacionalismo y Patria*, pp. 90–1.

[31] Alfredo Palacios: 'La F.O.R.A.' in *Nosotros*, XIV, No. 132 (1920).

[32] For Australia, see P. G. McCarthy: 'Labor and the Living Wage, 1890–1910', *The Australian Journal of Politics and History*, Vol. XIII, No. 1 (April 1967). The only period of large-scale unemployment in Argentina came during the First World War. In the 1920s the employment figures recovered rapidly and real wages went up considerably. (Di Tella and others, op. cit., pp. 342, 369, and 399).

[33] Quoted by H. O. Chalkey, Commercial Attaché to the British Embassy in

This attitude of the various Radical governments has been interpreted in a number of ways. Di Tella and Zymelman have suggested that the government could not possibly have gone against the vested interest of farmers and ranchers, a hypothesis which may well have something to do with the belief, widespread among our historians, that the weakness of successive Radical governments was a result of the fact that they opted for the constitutional way to political power (much against the wishes of their leader who hoped to reach it by revolutionary means). As we have pointed out earlier, Cornblit has made much of the lack of communication between the radical leadership and the immigrants. All these hypotheses help to illuminate certain extremely important aspects of our political history; particularly that outlined by Cornblit adds greatly to our understanding of certain *regional* characteristics of radicalism.[34] But in each case more attention is paid to marginal aspects of the problem under consideration, while the main reason that would explain why the Radical administrations should have adopted this particular policy is relegated to the background. It seems to us that the crux of the problem must be sought in the pressures brought to bear on these governments by their own electorate, firmly rooted in the new middle class of the Litoral and the Pampas. This attitude of the Radical electorate should be analysed in its economic and social context. It is pertinent to refer, therefore, to the peculiar structure of the so-called agrarian export sector.

The term 'agarian exporter' is frequently employed as a synonym for the great landowners, or more recently, for a coalition between these on the one hand and the big companies with foreign capital and the powerful traders based in the port of Buenos Aires who controlled the import-export business. In fact, the situation was rather more complicated than this use of the term 'agrarian export interest' suggests.

Again, the failure to stress sufficiently the phenomenon of expansion has given rise to an inadequate interpretation of reality. The rapid progress made in urbanization, in the fight against illiteracy and the advancement of the middle classes was not mirrored only in ever

---

Buenos Aires. *Parliamentary Papers, Overseas Trade Reports.* Session 10/2/1920 to 32/12/1920. Vol. XLII (1920).

[34] For example, in Córdoba the attitude of the Radicals was totally different, and only in the cases of Santa Fé and Buenos Aires itself could the 'Chauvinistic' attitude sometimes be found. See Ezequiel Gallo y Silvia Sigal, 'La Formación de los Partidos Políticos Contemporáneos. La U.C.R. 1890–1916' in *Desarrollo Económico*, Vol. III, No. 1–2 (Buenos Aires, 1964).

larger and more complex urban agglomerations. On the contrary, it had a profound effect on the rural panorama in the Pampas. Recently, Ruth Sautu has estimated that between 1869 and 1895 the part of the rural population that could be said to belong to the middle class went up from 17 per cent to 47 per cent.[35] An analysis of the two sets of census figures (1869 and 1914) relating to the provinces of Córdoba, Santa Fé, and Entre Ríos, reveals a similar process of growing complexity. In 1869 there were 11 towns with more than 2,000 inhabitants in these provinces; by 1914 there were 102 such towns.[36]

The figures quoted seem to reflect a rural panorama that was highly differentiated, with an extremely large middle-class element in it made up of landowners and tenant farmers, traders, transporters, etc. At the same time, the composition of the so-called 'upper classes' in the agrarian export sector underwent a parallel process of fragmentation.

There was bound to be a certain amount of conflict between these two sectors, which became more acute in years of crisis, and it is important for this to be taken into account, if our political history is to be interpreted correctly. Indeed, this conflict was more significant than any that was caused by the clash of interests of different sectors of the economy, such as that inherent in the agrarian-industrial dichotomy. But even in this context (and the reasons for it are more evident than in the case of the industrialists), tension and conflict were contained within a solid framework of concensus generated by the great economic expansion.[37]

These considerations are relevant to a fuller understanding of the attitude adopted by the Radical party with regard to the tariff problem. The Unión Cívica Radical was, above all, the fruit of the momentous upheavals that took place in the Pampas Litoral at this time. The Radical electorate consisted mainly of the new middle class that had sprung up in the towns and rural areas of this region, and were closely linked, as has been pointed out, to the agrarian export sector.[38] An electorate with these characteristics and with high hopes and aspirations encouraged by a favourable economic situation, was not of a kind to support a protectionist crusade. A more favourable attitude towards industry on the part of the radical leaders would not really have been

[35] These figures, which are a part of a study in preparation, were kindly given me by Ruth Sautu.
[36] Censos Nacionales of 1869 and 1914.
[37] See Cortés Conde y Gallo, passim.
[38] For the Radical electorate, see Gallo y Sigal, op. cit.

capable of modifying convictions so firmly held by a majority of the voters. And the support of the voters was essential for the first indigenous political party which organized itself with a view to the electoral struggle.[39]

IV. *Conclusions*

In this brief study I have attempted to point out some of the inadequacies and limitations that appear in recent works on the subject of the relationship between the agrarian and industrial sectors. Above all, I have tried to establish the fact that the behaviour of the various social sectors should be analysed within the context of the impressive economic and social expansion of that time. I am well aware of the extremely tentative and fragmented nature of this paper. Partly, this is because I am convinced that until more and more detailed monographs on the subject are available, the launching of new typologies would run the risk of imposing additional strait-jackets on investigation.

These considerations are particularly relevant in the case of the 'staple theory', which should, in my opinion, be regarded with some scepticism. On the one hand, the historical experience of Canada and Australia was not at all like that of Argentina, in spite of all the suggestive similarities that do exist. On the other hand, even the supporters of the 'staple theory' have admitted that it has weaknesses when confronted with more complex economic situations.[40]

Apart from this, however, we consider that the 'staple theory' provides the investigator with a useful tool for a first approach to problems of the kind we have discussed. Particularly useful in this case is the emphasis on the mechanism of propagating the process of growth in other branches of activity, and secondly the analysis of the complex social pattern which emerges as a result of economic expansion.

[39] Ibid. As late as 1939 the two main Radical leaders, Alvear and Sabatini, came out firmly in favour of preserving agrarian specialization. See *Hechos e Ideas*, 3/940, Jan. 1941, pp. 314–6 and 328–9. These ideas were of long standing in the party. Commenting on the 1912 electoral campaign the Argentine correspondent of *The Economist* wrote: 'The programme also pledges the [Radical] party "to endeavour to secure the gradual adoption of liberty of commerce, with ample interior and exterior competition of production and industry". There is no possibility that the Congress will consent to any change in its policy of protection of the so-called national industries . . . until the Radical and Socialist representation has been largely increased. . . .' See *The Economist*, 25 May 1912.

[40] See Kenneth Buckley, 'The Role of Staple Industries in Canada's Economic Development' and the subsequent discussion by Hugh G. J. Aitken, *The Journal of Economic History*, Vol. XVIII (No. 4, December 1958).

THE REVOLUTIONARY LEGION AND THE BRAZILIAN REVOLUTION OF 1930

by Peter Flynn

I. Introduction

HISTORIANS of the Brazilian revolution of October 1930 have been right to emphasize the divisions in the Liberal Alliance movement, which put Getúlio Vargas into power, and to stress the lack of any coherent programme for social and economic reform.[1] Even the *tenentes*, the young revolutionary officers so active throughout the 1920s, had, it is pointed out, no clear idea of what they wanted, beyond a general desire for change, linked to a deep-rooted suspicion of almost all politicians.[2] While, however, it is necessary to stress the divisions and incoherence of the revolutionary movement, there is, perhaps, a danger of carrying this too far, ignoring such programmes and formulae as the movement did produce, some of which have since lain neglected in private archives in Brazil.

The revolutionaries of 1930 did, after all, produce some blueprints for reform and took some steps to put them into execution and, without examining their crude attempts to formulate political, social, and economic aims, and the accompanying, equally primitive, efforts at party organization, it is difficult, for instance, to understand the political in-fighting leading to the São Paulo revolt of 1932 and the

---

[1] Barbosa Lima Sobrinho, *A Verdade sobre a Revolução de Outubro* (S. Paulo, 1933), pp. 93–103, 117–31. João Neves da Fontoura, *Memórias*, vol. II, *A Aliança Liberal e a Revolução de 1930* (Rio de Janeiro 1963), pp. 40, 481. Paulo Nogueira Filho, *Ideais e Lutas de um Burguês Progressista. O Partido Democrático e a Revolução de 1930*. 1 (2nd ed., Rio de Janeiro, 1965), pp. 368–71.

[2] Agildo Barata, *Vida de um Revolucionário* (Rio de Janeiro, n.d.), pp. 150–2. V. Santa Rosa, *O Sentido de tenentismo* (Rio de Janeiro, 1933), pp. 114. R. J. Alexander, 'Brazilian Tenentismo', *HAHR*, XXXVI (May 1956), 233–4. J. D. Wirth, 'Tenentismo in the Brazilian Revolution of 1930', ibid., XLIV (May 1964), 166–7. Barata again emphasized the lack of a specific tenente programme up to 1930 in conversation 21 Dec. 1965, as did Mauricio Goulart, 10 Feb. 1966.

intense bitterness of much of Brazilian politics throughout the 1930s. This is especially true at the local and state level, where personal vendettas and recriminations could affect political choices for many years. Again, a failure to study the political initiatives which collapsed within months of the October revolution makes an understanding of later developments, such as the right wing movement, *Integralismo*, all the more difficult.[3]

Above all, unless one sees why these initiatives failed, it is difficult to appreciate the problems facing those in 1930 who were anxious for reform, but found themselves against the entrenched power of the state political machines controlling the *coronelismo* system, that rule of local colonels or *chefes* who, traditionally, organized and controlled the vote, especially in rural areas.[4] The failure, in particular, of attempts at national political mobilization throughout the 1930s reveal the structural problems facing reformers in Brazil. They illustrate the lack of adequate civilian political structures at the national level and the conditions, therefore, for the steady development of political power by the one force capable of filling the vacuum, namely, the armed forces.

In this respect, perhaps, the most important and certainly the most neglected attempt at change was the effort of certain elements within the 1930 revolution to create what was virtually a national party of the revolution, first under the name of the Legion of October, or the Revolutionary Legion, later frankly accepting the title of National Revolutionary party (*Partido Revolucionário Nacional*). This was a deliberate attempt to break the coronelismo system, to replace narrow state loyalties by allegiance to a genuinely supra-state, national party of reform. What the Legion represented, what it aimed at and why it failed, is, therefore, an essential part of the story of the 1930 revolution and the politics of the early 1930s. Its neglect by historians is, consequently, all the more surprising.

Perhaps its quick collapse largely explains this neglect but, whatever the reason, almost nothing has been written about the Legion. The Legion

[3] Some of the attempts at revolutionary organization are mentioned briefly in Barata, op. cit., pp. 157–66. Also H. Silva, *1931. Os Tenentes no Poder* (Rio de Janeiro, 1966), pp. 74–7, 117–19. P. Nogueira Filho, op. cit., II. 594. Alexander, op. cit., pp. 236–7. Wirth, op. cit., pp. 173–7.

[4] The term *coronelismo* derives from the fact that the local landowner, the source of local political power and patronage, was usually, too, the colonel of the National Guard in his particular *município*. Cf. Victor Nunes Leal, *Coronelismo, Enxada e Voto. O Município e o Regime Representativo no Brasil* (Rio de Janeiro, 1948), pp. 7–12.

of October usually receives a mention in discussions of *tententismo*,[5] along with the revolutionary tribunal and the 3rd October Club,[6] but there is little attempt to link the club and the Legions or to examine the connections between, for instance, the tenentes and the more radical civilian politicians as revealed in these attempts at revolutionary organization. One reason may be that, while the 3rd October Club is usually described as a 'Jacobin Club',[7] or as a 'semi-official party' of the tenentes,[8] the Legion is more often defined in terms of its development in Minas Gerais where, under the influence of Francisco Campos, Gustavo Capanema, and Amaro Lanari, it moved more distinctly to the right than it did elsewhere.[9] But there is, obviously, a danger here of begging some important questions. One must beware, for instance, of defining the tenentes as Jacobins, men of the left, then ignoring the connections between them and phenomena such as the *Legião Mineira* or the attempts to form the National Revolutionary Party.[10] Conversely, it is difficult to see the Legion, as in Minas, merely as the attempt by Vargas to impose authoritarian government and destroy existing political parties,[11] while still viewing the 3rd October Club as the expression of 'revolutionary spirit'[12] or of tenente radical organization. There is need, in short, of a more coherent picture.

The aim here is simply to open up the question by examining the origins and some of the key ideas behind the Legions and then looking

[5] Cf. Wirth, op. cit., p. 173, when discussing the talks at Poços de Caldas.

[6] Ibid., p. 176; Alexander, op. cit., p. 236.

[7] V. Santa Rosa, op. cit., p. 144. Alexander, op. cit., p. 236.

[8] Wirth, op. cit., p. 176.

[9] So Wirth, op. cit., p. 171, especially note 24, referring to Afonso Arinos de Melo Franco, *Um estadista da República* (Rio de Janeiro, 1955), III. 1423 and 1489, says Minas Gerais, with its struggle between the *P.R.M.* (the Minas Republican Party) and Campos with 'his proto-fascist Legion of October' does not seem to have been a tenente sphere.

[10] A good example of this tendency is in Agildo Barata, op. cit., pp. 161–2. He describes the attempts to create a Revolutionary Legion exclusively in terms of the Minas example, modelled, he says, on German nazism and Italian fascism. The involvement of Juarez Távora and Miguel Costa in the Legion's organization embarrasses him, since it conflicts with the tenente insistence, as he sees it, on liberty. His claim that these were the only two tenentes involved is not accurate, nor his view that lack of tenente support caused the Legion's failure. In conversation (21 Dec. 1965) he insisted that the tenentes did not support right-wing movements, particularly, in later years, *Integralismo*.

[11] Mello Franco, op. cit., III. 1489–93.

[12] Alzira Vargas do Amaral Peixoto, *Getúlio Vargas. Meu Pai* (Rio de Janeiro, 1960), p. 79.

E

at their development and some of the reactions they produced in different states. In this respect, the case of Minas Gerais is particularly important; thus it will be discussed in more detail. This is not only because the Minas Legion is so often mentioned and so rarely examined but because the failure of the Legion in Minas—one of the three major states in Brazil—seems to illustrate the principal reason for its failure generally: namely, its swift absorption in the local political structure and its distortion in the interests of local party politics. The history of the Legion in Minas also affords a relatively rare example of Brazilian politics at their most intense, at the local, municipal level, and provides a clue to the nature of one of the most persistent political issues of the 1930s—the *caso Mineiro*. Because of this, and because the São Paulo question, for example, is being discussed elsewhere,[13] this paper concentrates on the reaction to the Legion in Minas Gerais as illustrating, to a large extent, its fate throughout the country.

II. *The divided alliance*

The announcement of the Legion began on 12 November 1930, the same day as Vargas's decrees instituting the provisional government and dissolving the national congress and the state and municipal assemblies. Aeroplanes over São Paulo dropped thousands of leaflets headed 'Manifesto to the People;'[14] it was signed by the tenente leaders, Miguel Costa, João Alberto, and Mendonça Lima, and it began by defining their position:

'The Revolution, now victorious in battle, must carry forward the work of national renewal. . . . The people made the revolution to be rid, once and for all, of the professional politicians. People of São Paulo'. Cooperate to assure the work of the revolution.'

This was already different from the assurance to the Paulistas on 26 October of Colonel Góes Monteiro, chief-of-staff of the revolutionary forces:

'The Vargas government will direct the Republic of the United States of

---

[13] In a book, now in preparation, *Brazil: From Revolution to Civil War 1929–1932. A Study of the Vargas Revolution of 1930 and the São Paulo Revolt of 1932.*

[14] The manifesto, published in the São Paulo press of 13 November, is printed in Nogueira Filho, op. cit., II. 738. For further details cf. ibid. 594–5. The *Estado de São Paulo* of 14 November had photographs of the Força Pública aeroplanes dropping the leaflets and on the 16, 19, and 25, it described the enthusiasm with which the Legion was greeted in the city.

Brazil with no other commitments than those contained in the Liberal Alliance programme.'[15]

Now, on 13 November, João Alberto, a young tenente representing the revolutionary government in São Paulo, told the São Paulo press of a new revolutionary organization, the Revolutionary Legion:

'The organisation of the Revolutionary Legion is the formula most needed for the urgent consolidation of the work of our revolution. This Legion is the result of an agreement which I have made with Juarez Távora, Oswaldo Aranha and the representative of Minas, all of them in full agreement with Sr. Getúlio Vargas. . . .'[16]

The programme of the Legion was essentially that of the Liberal Alliance, but he emphasized that, above all, he and his friends wanted 'to build a new Brazil, with a completely new mentality'. He went on:

'. . . It is possible that to some our organization will look like fascism. Nothing could be further from the truth. Fascism is a personalist absolutism, whereas our organization is radically anti-personalist, bound not to persons but to ideas. . . .'

Two days later came further news of the Legion when, on 15 November 1930, the *Diário de Notícias* carried headlines: 'The Legion of October—Oswaldo Aranha and Góes Monteiro, call for the enlistment of all who seek the glory of the Second Republic.' There was a long announcement of the formation of the Legion of October, followed by a manifesto signed by Aranha, as minister of Justice, and Góes Monteiro, as chief of general staff of the national forces.[17] The manifesto was headed by a quotation from Alberto Torres, the nationalist writer whose books—particularly *A Organização Nacional, O Problema Nacional Brasileiro* and *Fontes de Vida no Brasil*—had influenced some of the tenentes and younger revolutionaries:

[15] Ibid., II. 736.
[16] Ibid., II. 739.
[17] The original draft of this announcement, now in the Aranha Papers, is signed not only by Aranha and Góes, but, significantly, by two members of the military junta which had at first replaced President Washington Luís. These were Leite de Castro, Minister of War, and Isaías de Noronha, Minister of Marine. *Aranha Papers*, F.24, Ministério da Justiça, H a N. Diversos. Though the Aranha files are not numbered, F.24 (and similar numbers in references here) refers to a system I used when working in the archive, explained in an article on the Aranha papers soon to be published. I should here like to express my warmest gratitude to Dr. Euclydes Aranha Neto, the son of Dr. Oswaldo Aranha, for his permission to work in the archive and his extreme kindness to me while I did so.

'Brazilians have proved that they can be soldiers of the Republic: they must now show they can be citizens.'

Despite much rhetoric, the manifesto contained several important points. The enthusiasm of the revolution must now be harnessed for the work of reconstruction, hence the new organization of the Legion of October. This Legion must be nation-wide, not representing any one group; it is a civilian army to defend the revolution against all its enemies, and to realize the 'aspirations of the Brazilian spirit' proclaimed in the Liberal Convention and in the platform of the present head of the nation. But the manifesto also made it clear that the Legion's aims transcended those of the Alliance, working for 'a more profound transformation of the national life . . . with a much wider programme'. And this, it emphasized, must be done in a specifically 'Brazilian' manner (*brasileiramente*). Nor was the Legion a personalist movement, one seeking power for itself:

'It is not a political party, It has no electoral ambitions. . . . It sets out to co-operate with existing political parties, the autonomy of which it profoundly respects. . . .'

The Legion sought rather, said the manifesto, to work with existing groups for the good of Brazil as a whole, subordinating regional interests to the common good and providing a nation-wide organization, even in remote municipalities, to express, and educate, public opinion and the voice of the revolution.

Unfortunately, even in these first manifestos there was an inherent conflict between the aim to work for the structural reforms of Brazil and yet keep within the Liberal Alliance programme, just as there was between the stated intention to respect the existing—essentially local-political parties, yet create the Legion as a nation-wide, supra-regional organization. As it turned out, it was this second point which caused most trouble.

To understand why this was so and to appreciate the nature of the Legion's failure, it is important to remember just how divided was the movement which put Vargas into power. The Liberal Alliance was neither liberal nor an alliance. Embittered by squabbles over unpaid campaign expenses,[18] split by personal and party rivalry and unable

---

[18] Cf., for example, Aranha to Lindolfo Collor, 11 Feb. 1930, complaining of Minas Gerais not paying contributions. *Aranha Papers*, F.1, 5, Correspondência L. Collor. Especially, too, João Neves da Fontoura to Aranha, 27 Dec. 1929, ibid., F.46.

to agree on tactics or strategy, it was unworthy of the popular enthusiasm which it produced throughout Brazil.[19] Vargas himself was, right from the start, a most reluctant candidate for the opposition.

Rightly afraid of being another Nilo Peçanha,[20] and keenly aware of his debt to President Washington Luís, whom he had already served as minister of Finance, he much preferred his chances of receiving official government sponsorship for his candidature.[21] All his political instincts warned him against 'acting the role of Messiah'.[22] As the Alliance movement developed, he tried his best to avoid any clear commitment.[23] He was aware of the angry reaction of President Washington Luís as the opposition showed its hand:[24] hence his persistent attempts to reach a compromise solution rather than accept a direct confrontation. So, as late as December 1929, he made a secret arrangement with Washington Luís, in which he agreed to limit his electoral campaigning, and when, in the last days of that month, he broke this agreement, in order to campaign outside Rio Grande do Sul, he did so only with apologies to Washington Luís. Even then he failed to visit either Minas Gerais or Paraíba and only went to São

[19] On the popularity of the Vargas movement, cf. Nogueira Filho, op. cit., II. 405–7, 438. H. Silva, 1926: A Grande Marcha (Rio de Janeiro, 1965), pp. 401–7. Also cf. the United States State Department Files, 832.00, Revolutions, 54, Van de Arend (Pernambuco) 12 Oct. 1930; ibid., 832.00/74 from Porto Alegre (via Gade, Montevideo) 15 Oct. 1930; ibid. 832.00/147 Cameron (S. Paulo) 24 Oct. 1930; ibid. 832.00/218 Briggs (Bahia) 25 Oct. 1930.

[20] The governor of the state of Rio de Janeiro who had led the opposition to Artur Bernardes and whose state had later suffered from federal government reprisals.

[21] Cf. Flores da Cunha to Vargas, 29 Nov. 1928, Vargas Papers, November 1928. I should also like to express my sincere thanks to Dona Alzira Vargas do Amaral Peixoto, the daughter of President Vargas, for allowing me to use her father's papers and for advising and helping me in so many ways.

[22] Vargas to João Neves da Fontoura, 25 Nov. 1929: Vargas Papers, Nov.–Dec. 1929.

[23] See, for instance, his guarded reply in January 1929 to Antônio Carlos, the president of Minas Gerais and leader of the Liberal Alliance there. João Neves da Fontoura, Memorias, II. 53, and his reassuring letters to Washington Luís in January (Vargas Papers, 17 Jan. 1929) and again in May (ibid. 10 May 1929). This letter, like the earlier one to Washington Luís, was unknown to Borges de Medeiros and João Neves da Fontoura in June 1929 when the Gloria Pact was signed, committing Rio Grande do Sul and Minas to oppose Washington Luís—Lima Sobrinho, op. cit., p. 65.

[24] Vargas to Washington Luís, 11 July 1929, and Washington Luís to Vargas, 29 July 1929, Vargas Papers, July 1929.

Paulo when threatened with the desertion of the Paulista democrats if he refused.[25]

There was no fire or enthusiasm in his reading of the Alliance manifesto on the *morro do Castello* on 2 January 1930; he merely repeated the statements of the previous September and remained relatively unmoved by his enthusiastic reception on his short journey through São Paulo.[26] He, like Borges de Medeiros, Aranha and others who knew the electoral system, had realistically assessed his chances in the coming March election,[27] and he was aware that the cheers in São Paulo reflected more an opposition to the coffee policies of Washington Luís, and their probable continuation under his chosen successor, Júlio Prestes, than any deep commitment to the Liberal Alliance programme.[28]

The electoral defeat in March brought out still more clearly the divisions within the Liberal Alliance. Some of its members, who had primarily seen the Alliance as just another *ad hoc* electoral pact, believed that the struggle was now over. They agreed with the interview given by Borges de Medeiros, the powerful old leader of the Rio Grande do Sul Republican party, who argued that the presidential succession question was now closed.[29]

The more radical *Aliancistas* strongly disagreed. The electoral defeat, they argued, only showed more clearly the need for structural

[25] In this context cf. Vargas to João Neves, 27 Nov. 1929, *Vargas Papers*, Nov.–Dec. 1929.

[26] He still felt, as he had told Borges de Medeiros in a letter of 25 Nov. 1929— *Vargas Papers*, Nov.–Dec. 1929—that the door should be left open for reconciliation with Washington Luís: 'unfortunately events could move in a direction which neither you nor I want. . . .'

[27] Cf. Vargas to João Neves, 27 Nov. 29. *Vargas Papers*, Nov.–Dec. 1929. Also, Aranha to Neves 12 Dec. 1929, *Aranha Papers*, F.46, Correspondência, J. Neves: Neves had wired on 11 December that the coffee and financial situation was getting worse and so improving the Alliance's chances, if only its leaders kept a strong nerve. Aranha replied on 12 December that the changing financial position would not avoid electoral fraud and that 'Electoral victory is a fable from a *Thousand and One Nights*'. The difference between Aranha and Vargas was, of course, that Aranha was much more ready to turn to armed revolt once electoral victory seemed impossible.

[28] Though Vargas, like Aranha, did not think the coffee crisis could win him the election, he was aware of its political importance, as he showed in a letter to Neves of 25 Nov. 1929. *Vargas Papers*, Nov.–Dec. 1929. Excusing himself from going to the north-east at that time, he said it would be better to go later. This would allow time for Júlio Prestes to show his hand and 'besides, the coffee crisis will then have got worse'.

[29] *Correio do Povo*, 19 March 1930. *A Noite*, 19 March 1930.

reform. They bitterly attacked the Medeiros interview[30] and moved further towards alliance with the tenentes and preparations for armed revolt.

The tenentes, unfortunately, were also divided. Luís Carlos Prestes had broken with his former comrades and there was growing suspicion of the cynicism of some Aliancista politicians and their often excessive regionalism, irreconcilable with the tenentes' stress on *brasilidade*.[31] The conspiracy grew, but reports from the south emphasized the growing disunity and squabbling among the conspirators.[32]

The month of May brought the double blow of, first, the tragic drowning of Siqueira Campos, co-ordinator of the conspiracy in São Paulo,[33] then the manifesto of Luís Carlos Prestes, condemning the Alliance. Juarez Távora's reply showed how uncertain was the voice of tenentismo, so sadly hit by this double loss.[34]

At the end of May there was another shock, the eagerly awaited statement of Getúlio Vargas commenting on the March elections and the political situation. This seemed all too similar to the earlier interview of Borges de Medeiros, apparently trying to mollify rather than challenge the federal government.[35] The result was that by June 1930

[30] Cf. João Neves da Fontoura to Aranha on 17 March 1930, hoping to stop its publication. *Aranha Papers*, F.46. Correspondência. Also *Correio da Manha's* editorial 20 March 1930. For Borges de Medeiros's later qualifications of the interview, again to *A Federação* cf. *Correio da Manha* 26 March 1930.

[31] The regionalism comes out clearly in the Aranha files, as when after the start of the revolution seven members of the municipio of São Lourenço wired to Aranha on October 9, pledging support in his struggle for the *Riograndenisição da Patria*. *Aranha Papers*, F.31 Telegramas Recebidos, Revolução de 1930.

[32] Cf., for example, the reports of General Gil de Almeida, commander of the 3rd Military Division, to the Minister of War, Nestor Passos, now in the Aranha files. *Aranha Papers*, F.32, 3a. Região Militar, especially 9 Apr. 1930, 22 Apr. 1930, and 1 and 8 May.

[33] J. Alberto, op. cit., pp. 226–34. The shock of Siqueira's death is stressed in Glauco Carneiro, *O Revolucionário Siqueira Campos* (Rio de Janeiro 1966), II. 587–9.

[34] Prestes's manifesto and Tavora's reply are now printed in Nogueira Filho, op. cit., II. 710–18. Prestes's statement was immediately attacked by his former supporters—cf. editorial in *Correio da Manha* 30 May 1930. Also cf. editorial in *Diário da Manha* of Recife, of same date. This paper, and the *Diario da Tarde*, were both run by the Cavalcanti brothers, loyal friends of Prestes, who now, however, telegraphed to him expressing deep disappointment. Some of his friends, such as Dr. Tarquinio de Souza in Maranhão, at first refused to accept that the manifesto was the work of Prestes. Cf. too *Diário Nacional* of São Paulo 31 May 1930 on the disappointment felt by many, and the strings of protests in *Correio da Manha* throughout June.

[35] It was published in *Correio da Manha* of 1 June 1930, which described it in an editorial as 'a document more of gratitude than of protest', chiding Vargas for

the whole opposition movement seemed divided and demoralized. The Mineiros especially showed signs of giving up, even when Aranha assured them that adequate preparations were being made, including the organization of support among the federal forces in Minas Gerais. By June 28 another mineiro leader, Virgílio Mello Franco, could wire Aranha that all support had withered in Minas, so that he was determined 'to abandon this comedy'.[36]

Aranha, too, now seemed dispirited and beaten, for on 28 June, to the deep dismay of all the opposition, he abruptly resigned his position as secretary of Justice for Rio Grande do Sul.[37] This, it appeared, marked the irrevocable break-up of the revolutionary conspiracy, first disowned by its political leaders, then condemned by the chief of tenentismo and now abandoned by its principal organizer.

The crisis was, in fact, more apparent than real, since what Aranha had told Campos was still true. The conspiracy was still going on, even quickening now that Aranha had more time to give to it. The Aranha papers for this period contain frequent telegrams between Aranha and the federal garrisons, especially in the south.[38] He had detailed lists of arms and personnel in all the garrisons of the *Brigada* (the state force) in Rio Grande do Sul,[39] and there are lists of federal officers, including those in Minas, showing those who favoured the revolution, those against, and those indifferent.[40] The letters from

---

failing to attack the Washington Luís government, especially over its treatment of Paraíba; Vargas, to do him justice, had, in fact, rebuked the federal government over this. Also, while saying the campaign was now closed, he made the significant qualification: '. . . it is now up to the people to say whether or not they agree with this closure'.

[36] Cf. Francisco Campos to Aranha 17 June 1930 and 21 June 1930, expressing the grave doubts of the Minas president, Antonio Carlos, about the feasibility of revolution. *Aranha Papers*, F.31, Revolução 1930.

[37] A typical reaction was that of João Neves, to whom the news seemed to come as a complete surprise. He sent an urgent coded wire to Aranha on the 28th: 'Bewildered. What is it? Camouflage or disagreement? Peace or war? . . .' *Aranha Papers*, F.31, Telegramas Recebidos.

[38] Cf. especially *Aranha Papers*, F.31 Revolução de 1930, *passim*. Typical, for instance, is a report from Quim Cesar from Passo Fundo 20 August 1930, saying the garrison is all ready for revolt and giving details of the arms available.

[39] There is, for example, a list of personnel in the *Brigada* of Rio Grande do Sul, dated 26 July 1930, *Aranha Papers*, F.32, Revolução de 1930, diversos, and the list of arms held by the Brigada, dated 18 Aug. 1930, and of personnel as distributed throughout all the different municípios, ibid. There are also lists of the *Provisorios* ibid.

[40] Ibid. cf. list of revolutionary officers in Minas Gerais and in Rio Grande, 15 Sept. 1930.

General Gil de Almeida also reflect continuing activity among known tenente conspirators.[41]

Through all this critical period, Aranha held the conspiracy together, so that when in July 1930 the murder of João Pessoa in Paraíba gave new impetus to the movement, he and his friends had already provided the revolutionary organization to take advantage of the emotional upsurge.

In terms of developments after November 1930 it is, however, important to notice how the divisions in the Liberal Alliance movement persisted even after the murder of João Pessoa in July. So, for instance, on 28 August 1930, Raul Pilla wrote to Aranha complaining that, though revolution was imminent, he, as leader of the *Partído Libertador*, the other major party together with the Republican party in Rio Grande do Sul, knew none of the details, since decisions were being made only by the Republicans:

'I cannot see in all this anything else but a scheme to deprive the Libertador Party of all influence and transform it into a mere lackey of the revolution, or, indeed, to ruin it completely by absorbing its most active elements.'[42]

On 16 September, Rubens Maciel, a *gaucho* ally, sent a most disquieting letter from Pelotas. There is evidence, he says, of a plot by Borges de Medeiros and Vargas to betray the Libertadores and the 'left wing' of the revolutionary movement:

'What alarms Borges is the formidable advance of the Libertadores and the split in his own party.'[43]

He reports fears that the old revolutionaries and the 'left wing' will commit the state to revolution, though inadequately prepared, simply to justify the expenses so far incurred. Whatever the substance of these rumours, the very fact that they could circulate is evidence of the general atmosphere of distrust and suspicion.

Indeed, even after the revolution had started, the same divisions persisted. On 5 October, for example, Glycério Alves wired to Vargas from Cachoeira, saying that the day before he had been with Borges on his *fazenda* in the interior of Rio Grande do Sul, where he lived in virtual retirement. Pleased with the revolution, Borges nevertheless showed much *preoccupação partidária* (these words being

[41] Ibid., 3a. Região Militar, especially 9 April onwards.
[42] *Aranha Papers*, F.32, Correspondência Recebida.
[43] Ibid.

underlined). Borges therefore strongly recommended that the Republican forces should be organized under their own party chefes, as in the past, leaving the Libertadores to organize their own followers. The last two lines of the letter are in red ink and especially worth noting:

'In all events, it is most desirable that the predominance of our party should be guaranteed.'[44]

One of the most severe disagreements of all came right at the end, over how to react to the take-over by the military junta on 24 October. Juarez Távora telegraphed on the 24th expressing his fear that the revolution might be betrayed by false friends.[45] Góes saw a similar danger,[46] and Aranha's own brother, Luís, wired to Oswaldo from Porto Alegre that he feared lest, at this very last moment, the revolution might be betrayed.[47] On the eve of victory, it seemed, the doubts and divisions were as serious as ever—a fact always to be remembered in evaluating post-revolutionary developments.

These particular fears were, as it turned out, groundless, since neither Vargas nor Aranha had any intention of compromising with the military junta or of handing over the revolution to them. The more serious question, however, once power was secured, was what the revolution really stood for. It had now outgrown its origins as an essentially personalist, opportunistic political alliance. It had been adopted reluctantly, almost apologetically, by the man who was now being made head of the provisional government. It had been achieved less through the strength of the revolutionaries than through the weakness of the central government and, especially, the fatal obstinacy of Washington Luís. It was coming to power seriously divided and with a major crisis—the question of São Paulo—already taking shape. Worst of all, the revolutionaries, now in charge, had no clear, detailed programme of revolutionary government and administration.

This really was the crux of the matter. The only programme so far revealed was that of September 1929[48] and of Vargas's speech of 2 January 1930 on the Esplanada do Castelo, repeated, with varying emphasis, by him and by Liberal Alliance speakers throughout the country. But the Liberal Alliance programme was less a blue-print

[44] *Aranha Papers*, F.32, Correspondência Recebida. A–L.

[45] *Aranha Papers*, F.31, Telegramas Recebidos.

[46] Ibid., Góes to Colonel Lúcio Esteves and cf., Góes to Aranha 23 Oct. 1930, ibid. and 25 Oct. 1930, ibid.

[47] Ibid. '. . . the least concession would be a crime'.

[48] Part of the September manifesto can be found in Nogueira Filho, op. cit., II. 693–8.

for government than a rallying-cry for opposition to Washington Luís.[49] The Alliance programme, as outlined by Vargas, contained something for everybody. It tried to recognize and conciliate every interest in Brazil, the dominant economic groups in every region, industrialists as well as agriculturalists, importers as well as exporters, the critics of coffee valorization and the coffee interests wanting defence. It aimed to satisfy young tenente rebels, angry over promotion blocks and unsatisfactory service conditions, while, at the same time, making promises to senior serving officers. Vargas promised a new deal both for urban and rural workers, yet proposed his reforms so as to least offend both landowners and employers. He agreed with critics of the public administration system, yet made suggestions as how best to benefit officials then in office. He urged constitutional reform and the free vote as a remedy for Brazilian ills, yet carefully acknowledged the demand to adapt the political and administrative system to the conditions of the country. He even managed, as spokesman of the Alliance campaign and leading critic of Washington Luís, to find praise for the latter's financial policies and give some guarantee that, in essentials, they should continue.

Yet, because of the way the revolution developed, the Vargas speech of 2 January 1930 and the manifesto of the previous September remained the only major statements of Alliance aims and policies. Granted the divided nature of the Alliance movement and its stumbling, uncertain road to power, it was inevitable that deep disagreements must now arise as to what the revolution should do. Already the Alliance had achieved what for many, such as the mineiro president, Antônio Carlos, was its primary aim, the removal of Washington Luís and the blocking of Júlio Prestes as his successor. For others, gauchos like Raul Pilla, for instance, or Assis Brasil, there was little more to do, except arrange for new elections and guarantee constitutional government. But for the real organizers of the revolution, especially Aranha, the more reformist politicians and the spokesmen of tenentismo, the work of the revolution was just beginning, which leads again to the Legion of October and the manifesto of 15 November 1930.

III. The legions

No one so far has investigated the origins of the Legions or the ideas which were being shaped in those confused weeks and months before and after the revolution. It is difficult (since most of the meetings

[49] The manifesto is published in Vargas, *A Nova Política do Brasil* (Rio de Janeiro), I. 19–54.

were private and unrecorded) to chart the growth of the Legion in those early days. João Neves, however, describes a meeting of revolutionaries at Aranha's house on the morning of either 14 or 15 November 1930 when, he says, the 'precursors of the 3rd October Club' were already demanding a revolutionary programme of Aranha and Juarez Távora.[50] A recent study of the period, mentioning the contemporary disenchantment with democratic government, talks of the hopes of most of the younger revolutionaries of starting a national revolutionary party when organizing the Legions, and of the opposition of many writers and intellectuals to the October revolution.[51] Silva describes how Aranha called a meeting at his house of young intellectuals.[52]

They were received informally by Aranha and Plínio Salgado was introduced by Alfredo Egídio as 'the man who can provide a programme for the revolution'. Aranha, busy organizing the Legion of October in Rio, had Italian fascist books open on his desk and, in discussion about who should be the national head of the Legion, he favoured Captain Frederico Cristiano Buys, a young officer much influenced by European fascism.[53] Plínio Salgado, principal author of the manifesto of the Revolutionary Legion of São Paulo, spoke for the Paulista Legion, and it was agreed that contact should be made with Francisco Campos, then forming the Legion in Minas Gerais. Campos joined the same group a few days later in the Palace Hotel for another meeting and they later met again in the offices of A Noite, setting up a secretariat general for the Legion. They were joined by Professor Raul Bittencourt and Otávio de Faria, and there was prominent display of more fascist literature and pictures of Mussolini.[54] It seems, however, that it was this meeting which split the group. Raul Bittencourt proposed, what seems to have been perfectly acceptable to all present, a body equivalent to the fascist

[50] João Neves da Fontoura, Accuso! (Rio de Janeiro, 1933), pp. 19–20.

[51] H. Silva, 1931. Os Tenentes no Poder (Rio de Janeiro, 1966), pp. 74–5.

[52] These included Augusto Frederico Schmidt, Francisco Clementino de San Tiago Dantas, Gilson Amado, Chermont de Miranda, Antônio Gallotti, Américo Jacobina Lacombe, Hélio Miranda, and Aranha's cousin, Alfredo Egídio Aranha. Lacombe seems to have been Silva's main source for the events described. These accounts also complement information received in conversations with Agildo Barata (21 Dec. 1965) who said the Legion was launched by Aranha at his home, and with Plínio Salgado (20 Dec. 1965) who said the Integralista movement was really started in Aranha's house.

[53] Silva, op. cit., p. 76.

[54] Ibid., p. 77.

grand council and the break came when discussing its membership.[55]

These meetings are interesting as revealing Aranha's early attempts at revolutionary organization and his anxiety to bring former critics of the revolution into the work of reconstruction which he envisaged. They are evidence, too, of the inchoate nature of the revolutionary programme, with Aranha casting around for ideas and supporters, willing even to waste time in fruitless discussions with incorrigible doctrinaires. The refusal of Schmidt, Salgado, and the others, to associate themselves with the Vargas revolution is also worth noticing. Salgado later tried with Integralism to provide a political organization more suited, as he believed, to the peculiar needs of Brazilian society.

Meanwhile, however, Aranha and others were still trying to build up the Legions, to give the revolution the content, organization, and united sense of purpose which it so conspicuously lacked. Their private discussions went unrecorded, but it is possible to attempt some description of the programmes and schemes by relying on the series of manifestos then published and, more useful still, on certain draft formulae to be found in the Aranha and Vargas papers.

A succint summary of the Legion's ideas is difficult, since they consist mostly of plans and projects which are often inconsistent or irreconcilable. They are an amalgam, for the most part, of tenente sentiment, the programmes of the São Paulo Democrats and the Liberal Alliance, joined now to newer notions taken from European fascism or stimulated by the economic crisis. One sees, too, the influence of Brazilian authors, notably Alberto Torres, Oliveira Vianna, Olavo Bilac, Graça Aranha, and Euclides da Cunha. Too often all are mixed together with little thought of consistency or coherence, and they constantly threaten to decline into pretentious nonsense. Nevertheless, the search through the archives is worth the

[55] Bittencourt argued that membership should be limited to those who had worked actively in the October revolution, but Augusto Frederico Schmidt strongly disagreed. The impression, he said, in the meetings with Aranha was not that he and his friends were being asked to identify themselves with the revolution, but that they were starting something new:'We all [and he spoke for all] resisted the revolution and do not now regret it. . . .' Schmidt and his friends then withdrew, Plínio Salgado returned to São Paulo and later directed *A Razão* with Alfredo Egídio Aranha and San Tiago Dantas, who soon joined Francisco Campos at the Ministry of Education. Silva, op. cit., p. 77. On 14 February, Alfredo Egídio wrote to Oswaldo, explaining his aim, according to principles which he had worked out with Plínio Salgado, to start a newspaper to instruct the Brazilian élites in the ideas of the revolution, to give the people a 'sense of construction' and a 'feeling of integral nationalism' (*nacionalismo integral*). *Aranha Papers*, F.23, Ministério da Justiça. Recebidos.

trouble, revealing, besides the confusion and uncertainty of the new regime, the enthusiasm and zeal for reform of many of its younger, more optimistic, supporters.

Oswaldo Aranha's personal role is unmistakable. His aim, as he later said, was to organize the victory as he had organized the revolution,[56] and many of the ideas behind the Legion can be found in speeches by Aranha going back as far as December 1916. Certainly all the evidence suggests that Aranha, at this stage, was the principal inspiration.[57]

The Aranha files reinforce this picture of Aranha moulding the Legion. Some of the schemes to be found there were drafted before the October revolution of 1930. One such, dated Porto Alegre, 16 September 1930, and headed *A Revolutionary Plan for Brazil*, stresses the need, once victory is won, to prevent the armed forces imposing a military dictatorship.[58] This is interesting, since it would explain Aranha's description of the Legion in November as a 'civilian army' and Borges's statement in his letter of 31 March that Aranha and Campos founded the Legion to counter the threat of military government.[59] Another pre-revolution document, typewritten and unsigned, is under ten headings.[60] It introduces the socio-economic and moralistic elements in the subsequent Legionary programmes:

[56] Cf. his speech when handing over the Ministry of Justice to Maurício Cardoso, 21 December 1931: 'I, for my part, gave myself to the organization of victory with the same enthusiasm as I had worked for the revolution.' *Aranha Papers*, F.17, Discursos, 1931.

[57] Salles Filho, writing in March 1931, refers to Aranha's early hopes of founding a *Legião Carioca*. (*Aranha Papers*, F.23, Ministério da Justiça, 6 March 1931) Borges de Medeiros, in a letter of 31 March, speaks of Aranha and Campos as the founders of the Legion, and Miguel Costa, writing to Vargas on 29 July, says the Legion was founded by order of Aranha and Góes Monteiro (*Vargas Papers*, Julho–Dezembro 1931, p. 13). In September Mauricio Goulart, inviting Aranha to attend the first Congress of the São Paulo Legion, speaks of him as inspiring it (*Aranha Papers*, F.23, 17 Sept. 1931, and 10 Oct. 1931), as does Mendonça Lima on 10 October. Other witnesses, too, see Aranha as the force behind the Legion, as when, on 12 March 1931, the United States Military Attaché in Brazil, reported: 'The driving force behind this new political party is undoubtedly Oswaldo Aranha . . . unquestionably the strongest man in the provisional administration and the one exerting the most compelling influence over the nominal chief of the government and over public affairs in general. . . .' He went on to suggest that, if the Legion were to become a truly national organization, it would probably be used to eliminate and replace Vargas. (U.S. State Department, 832.00/718).

[58] *Aranha Papers*, F.32, Revoluçao de 1930.

[59] *Aranha Papers*, F.23, Ministério da Justiça.

[60] *Aranha Papers*, F.32, Revolução. Exposições e Planos de . . .

(1) *Temperance*—Complete prohibition of alcoholic drinks.

(2) *Gambling*—Absolute prohibition of games of chance, including lotteries.

(3) *Land*—Sequestration of private estates. The land is the property of the nation. The occupier must be considered only as a tenant.

(4) *Territory*—Fusion of small states into one much bigger state. Much greater economy. Example: Paraná and Santa Catharina, etc.

(5) *Congress*—Extinction of the chambers and their substitution by technical councils, nominated by the president, which function only when summoned.

(6) *Women*—Prohibition of women in public offices, except those of health and education.

(7) *Morality*—Prohibition of brothels. War on immorality. He cannot be a good citizen who is not a good head of the family.

(8) *Illness*—Retirement or pensioning off of all employees unfit for service, whether for physical reasons (lameness, blindness, tuberculosis, etc.), or for moral unsuitability.

(9) *Justice*—Unification of justice.

(10) *Elections*—Universal suffrage only in the município, for municipal offices. For all others limited suffrage—by the representatives of the município for state elections and by the representatives of the state for national elections.

Another scheme, signed Wuerth, November 1930,[61] is entitled: *Plano Ideal de um Fascismo Brasileiro—The Dictatorship of Good over Evil*. Under a sub-heading of *Scheme for Organization of the Brazilian National Legion*, it outlines the structure of the movement: a supreme head of the Legion, military chief, secretary general, chief-of-staff; a supreme council, state councils, regional councils; local chiefs, and local militias. It describes its purpose as being to build centres for the spread of national and civic culture and proposes various means. The total result will be 'the mobilization of all individual effort and initiative to promote the good, the progress, the security, order, justice and harmony of the whole of Brazil'.

A similar scheme in the same file[62] is much longer and more detailed. It is in two main parts, the first of which provides for a permanent administrative body attached to the Ministry of Justice. Its first duty

[61] *Aranha Papers*, F.32, Informaõzes e Boletins. I have not yet been able to find out who Wuerth was.

[62] Ibid.—Esqueleto do Serviço.

must be to watch and control all those suspected of being counter-revolutionaries, to take care of political prisoners, fugitives, communist leaders, their agents, and others who are listed as being a threat to the revolution. There should be massive propaganda, which will depend to a great extent on the popularization of the radio in rural areas and the formation of cells to stimulate patriotic duty and hard work among the masses (in brackets 'Facismo' [sic]) and the mobilization of teachers, ministers of religion, journalists, and writers.

The second part of the same plan for the Legion gives details of the structure of the organization. There will be need of regional chiefs and investigators and, in some cases, spies, informants, and men to handle censorship. This second organization, the scheme suggests, will be in the hands of a supreme chief, Dr. Oswaldo Aranha, and 'should have ramifications throughout the whole of Brazil. (Fascism)...'

Other documents in these files propose similar or alternative schemes. One, dated Rio, 24 October 1930, headed 'The Revolutionary Programme',[63] describes what should be the structure of the government and outlines its most urgent tasks, notably the wide increase in power of the central government. This includes dissolution of national and state congresses and the setting-up of a body to revise federal and state laws and constitutions, making them uniform for the whole of Brazil.

These were only some of the projects and plans being discussed as Aranha and his friends began the work of shaping the Legion. Already the ideas expressed were going far beyond the Liberal Alliance programme, so it is worth noting that, though the main drive and inspiration came from Aranha, he was supported by most of the more radical politicians and the leading spokesmen of tenentismo. This is a point to emphasize since later, when the revolutionary movement was split over the São Paulo question, Aranha was accused of being almost solely responsible for starting the Legion and exacerbating the Paulista crisis. Among those who said this was Baptista Luzardo, when he and other gaucho politicians broke with the Vargas government in March 1932, but Aranha could then remind him that Luzardo, too, had been closely involved in the early organization of the Legion.[64]

Closely linked, in Aranha's mind, to the growth of the Legion was the build-up of the 3rd October Club, which he also helped to found.

[63] *Aranha Papers*, F.32, Revoluçao de 1930.
[64] *Aranha Papers*, F.32, Revolução 1930, where Aranha also explains that he helped to form the Minas Legion to strengthen the 'civil power' in Brazilian politics, but then disagreed with the direction it took under Campos.

To him in 1930 there was none of that contradiction which some historians have seen between a radical 'Jacobin' Club and a right-wing, authoritarian, Legion. Aranha gave his view of the Club much later, in March 1932, when he finally broke with it. He then told its president, Pedro Ernesto:

'The 3rd October Club was founded to harmonize, coordinate and defend the ideas of the revolutionaries of October, coming from all sectors of opinion in Brazil, both civilian and military. I helped to found it, because I thought there was need of this work of consolidation, refinement and organization of the revolutionary movement.'[65]

Aranha, by that stage, deplored the domination of the Club by one faction, the tenentes, contrary to the interests of the revolution and Brazil.[66]

Aranha's interpretation of the Club and of the Legion were part of his general concept of the revolution, frequently expressed in his correspondence and speeches, one of his more important statements being in a speech he made on 21 December 1931, when welcoming the new Minister of Justice, Mauricio Cardoso.[67] This, he said, was 'the era of the moral and material reconstruction of Brazil'. On the question of constitutional rule, he stressed that, while extraordinary powers might at first be needed, as expressed in Decree No. 19.398[68] of 11 November 1930, the revolution was committed to ruling constitutionally. Examining his time at the Ministry of Justice, he then went on:

'My aim was to give shape to the Revolution, organizing the Brazilian communities within a new order, and making it impossible for a defeat of the central government to destroy the work of the revolution. . . . This, too, was exactly my intention in creating the Legion, the aim of which was the organization of the civilian power and that of all the revolutionaries. . . . . I was beaten and applauded only for my defeat. . . .'

Time and again comes the same idea, to organize the revolution and prevent a take-over by its enemies, to provide a framework and

[65] Ibid. Correspondência Expedida.

[66] He told Pedro Ernesto on this occasion his views, and repeated them to Flores da Cunha on 30 March 1932 (*Aranha Papers*, F.15, Correspondência Expda.) and again to Antunes Maciel in June (F.32, Revolução 1932).

[67] *Aranha Papers*, F.17, Discursos 1931. The speech was published in 1932, but I have only been able to find it in Aranha's archive. There is clear need for an edition of Aranha's speeches, as there is of a good biography.

[68] Nogueira Filho, op. cit., II. 741-3.

F

formula for revolutionary government and genuine reconstruction, not to allow elections too quickly, lest they should merely prevent this aim. The speech provides one of the most important contemporary analyses of the revolution of October and the problems of the new government.

Equally important, in the present context, is the coincidence of its key ideas—the *eventual*, but not the immediate re-constitutionalization of the country and the prior need for genuine reconstruction—with those expressed in, for instance, the manifesto of the 3rd October Club of 27 December 1931.[69] By then, of course, the Legion had proved a failure and Aranha was disillusioned with the Club, but the initial identity of purpose must be accepted, as must the involvement of tenente leaders in the early organization of the Legion.[70]

The first announcements and manifestos of the Legion in November 1930 have already been mentioned. Between their appearance and that of the São Paulo Legion's manifesto on 3 March 1931 there were many long discussions over the shape the Legions should take, discussions which are also reflected in the Aranha and other archives. Some are primarily concerned with the structure of the Legion, such as the scheme for the Legion in São Paulo.[71] The state of São Paulo is to be divided into ten zones, corresponding to the electoral districts under the old regime. The regional centres of the Legion will be the cities of greatest importance and the state capital will be one zone and head of the Legion in São Paulo. There will be a regional director in every zone and a municipal director in every município. Every municipal Legion is to have a deliberative council of three members, whose duties are also set out. These will come under a central committee in São Paulo to whom they must report regularly. The document ends with an interesting definition of those who may become Legionaries, namely, every citizen who shows that he is over eighteen years old, that he is Brazilian born, that he has the physical and mental capacity for some employment, that he does not suffer from infectious or contagious disease, that he is of good character, is in full agreement

[69] Printed in Paulo Nogueira Filho, *Ideais e Lutas de um Burguês Progressista—A Guerra Cívica 1932*. (Rio de Janeiro, 1965) I. 406–7.

[70] Another unpublished document in the Aranha files is a long statement, undated and unsigned, but headed 'Directives for the Organization of the General Staff of the 3rd October Club'. *Aranha Papers*, F.24, Ministério da Justiça. This, too, stresses the need to provide a disciplined organization to safeguard the work of the revolution. One major difference, however, between this and the Legions' draft statements is the frequent quotations here from Marx, Engels, and Lenin.

[71] *Aranha Papers*, F.32, Ministério da Justiça.

with revolutionary thought, and is disposed to the strictest obedience to orders coming from the hierarchical superiors of the Legion.

Another paper in the same file is heades: *Bases for Drafting a Proclamation to launch the National Revolutionary Party (The Legion of October).*[72] It is an interesting and important draft, not only because it now speaks of the Legion as a 'National Revolutionary Party' and for what it reveals of some of the basic ideas behind it, but because it provoked a memorandum, also preserved, from one of the leading theorists of the Legion, Captain Frederico Cristiano Buys. In this draft and the Buys memorandum, one can see something of the debate which went into the Legion's manifestos. The author of the draft proclamation suggests that they should start by declaring that the Revolutionary Party (P.R.N.) is formed to carry out the work of the revolution, not to support the members of the Provisional Government, who must resign or be removed from office should they fail to meet the nation's demands. Then should follow an absolutely honest examination of the state of the country, under various heads:

'(a) *Financial*—the federal, state and municipal finances. How much we owe abroad. But this should be expressed in Brazilian currency, so that the people can clearly understand why we are demanding such sacrifices. (b) *Economic*— show the anarchic and outdated nature of the Brazilian economy, with its lack of scientific organization. The slavery of our economy to the coffee economy. Every activity in the country is immediately or indirectly subordinated to the salvation of coffee. The dangers and errors of this policy.[73] (c) *Social*—The anarchy and lack of organization in Brazilian society. Predominance of some classes over others. Dangers of this. [Then, added in pencil, possibly by Aranha,][74] Education, Hygiene, Instruction. Organization of labour under its various aspects. (d) *Political*—Democracy is contrary to the federal structure. Democracy implies dismemberment. What is needed . . . a unitary régime, temporary dictatorial government, strengthening of the idea of the One, Indivisible Nation. Guarantee of *brasilidade*. Political centralisation. Administrative decentralisation. (e) *Administrative* . . . Too many badly paid civil servants. Need to simplify the machine. Impose a minimum wage and a new law of promotions, retirement and pensions. The State must provide pensions for its employees, setting up an Institute, under direct state control for this purpose.'

[72] *Aranha Papers*, F.32, Ministério da Justiça.
[73] This passage, like those criticizing a democratic system for Brazil, was bound to bring reaction in São Paulo, especially from the Democratic Party. It is worth noticing in this respect that this draft immediately follows another in the file, which begins: 'Brazilians! Brazil was a democratic fraud' and goes on strongly to attack democracy.
[74] The note seems to be in Aranha's handwriting.

Then comes sections on education and public instructions, stressing the importance of technical education, and the problem of adult illiteracy. The draft ends by defining its political position:

'. . . Only a strong Government can carry out such a programme. Need of a Dictatorship and foundation of the P.R.N. The old pre-Revolutionary parties could never succeed in bringing back Brazil to the lines of its evolution. All of them regionalist, they were concerned only with themselves, their men, their own states, and hardly ever with the Nation as a whole. The old parties recognised the wider Nation only in showing resistance to the central power. . . The National Revolutionary Party is turning from destruction to construction. Conserve what is good. Improve what is imperfect. Destroy what is prejudicial.'

This was strong stuff, very different from Góes Monteiro's promise to the Paulistas on 26 October[75] and, in its remarks on the political parties, far removed from the manifesto of 15 November, with its talk of co-operation.[76]

The draft seems to have been debated in detail by the revolutionaries, for next to it in this file comes a long comment on it by Frederico Cristiano Buys. Essentially this is a word of warning. These ideas, he says,[77] unless carefully presented, can easily rebound to destroy the Legion. Indeed, he thinks that the Legion's failure will be certain unless its leaders tread very carefully, especially with regard to the existing political parties:

'Mere affirmation is not proof, and it is little use saying that the Legion has no political ambitions or is not a political party when, quite clearly, this is not true. . . .'

A wiser course is to admit, frankly, that the Legion aims to become a national revolutionary party:

'Let us call our party by its real name, the National Revolutionary Party. . . .'

Buys makes reference to foreign precedents, to Primo de Rivera and the Patriotic Union in Spain, and to the National Union in Portugal, saying that one must expect every resistance from old parties in refusing to be eaten up and absorbed, especially from the Republican and Libertador parties in Rio Grande do Sul and the Republican

[75] See above, pp. 64–5.
[76] See above, p. 66.
[77] *Aranha Papers*, F.32, Ministério da Justiça.

party in Minas Gerais.[78] Aranha, it seems, agreed with him on the difficulties in Rio Grande do Sul. He has scribbled in pencil in the margin: 'é a espinha dorsal' (the backbone of the whole thing), adding:

'If the Partido Republicano supports en masse the new Revolutionary Party, the Partido Libertador will withdraw. And vice versa. A historical certainty, a tradition which one must change—but not abruptly.'

This was Buys's central argument—the relations with the existing political parties:

'I consider the P.R.N. must annihilate all existing parties in the country.'

He even presented a long argument showing that the São Paulo Democratic Party, which had supported the Revolution, was a fraud, representing the same vested interests as the São Paulo Republican party, acting merely as its left-wing. The gaucho parties in Rio Grande do Sul, too, were incorrigibly regionalist, concerned only with their petty squabbles. None of the parties could achieve the aims of the revolution, hence the need for their elimination and a new National Revolutionary Party.

This, of course, revealed the basic issue lying behind all the new programmes and schemes which were being drawn up—the reaction from the existing political parties—above all, from those politicians who, in Rio Grande do Sul, Minas and São Paulo, had supported the Liberal Alliance and the revolution, but whose concept of it was so different from that of the Legionaires. By March 1931, when the São Paulo manifesto appeared, it was clear that the challenge was already being taken up.

The *Manifesto of the Revolutionary Legion of São Paulo*, published on 4 March 1931, was described by the United States consul in São Paulo at the time as 'the first formal effort to state the revolutionary aims comprehensively'.[79] This was, in fact, a fair description, which

---

[78] '. . . We shall meet the strongest resistance in Rio Grande do Sul, with its two parties, the Republican and Libertador, and in Minas and with the P.R.P. (S. Paulo Republican Party). The P.D. [Democratic Party of S. Paulo] has only a formal existence and that of the Federal District is a fiction. The North will resist because of the ignorance and lack of political education of the masses. Still, since there are no parties in that region, the idea of the foundation of the P.R.N. will be well received and the party will take root. . . .' This, as the Legionaries later found out, was a dangerous underestimation of the Democratic Party.

[79] U.S. State Department. 832.00/717—Cameron. S. Paulo 7 March 1931.

makes the Paulista manifesto an important document and well worth studying. Since, however, it is readily available, it hardly needs to be examined in detail here.[80] It makes its appeal to all classes and occupational groups, based on a series of Fundamental Principles, including the definition of the 'Brazilian social type' and 'the Brazilian man'. There is emphasis on a strong state and a greatly enlarged central power, but it is made clear that the powerful state exists only to serve the individual—'We seek the good of the whole individual'.[81] The manifesto declares 'war on the private latifundio' and on trusts and monopolies, and 'the absorption of the national patrimony by foreign syndicates', and there is a long section called 'Against All Imperialisms', which is described as 'the supreme national defence'.

The nationalist idea of 'brasilidade' dominates the manifesto, with its reference to authors such as Alberto Torres,[82] and Euclides Aranha. The aim is to face up to Brazil's specific problems, finding equally specific Brazilian answers, solving them 'brasileiramente', as the manifesto of the previous November had put it. There should be no more reliance on foreign, imported political systems, such as the English parliamentary system followed until 1889. Foreign models, whether from the United States, Italy, or Russia, were unsuited to Brazil.[83] So there must be *Brazilian* laws and a *Brazilian* constitution.

Increased state power will only be used for the good of individuals and the family and to defend the 'rights of Brazilian man'. The individual is prior to the state, so that the dictatorship of any one class is also contrary to human rights. The state must intervene in the economic life of the nation, to stimulate and control initiative, direct and co-ordinate production, and see to the needs of labour, such as the minimum wage, but all in the interest of the individual. Other sections deal with the Federation, where the power of the states needs to be curbed, with consequent strengthening of the central government, and with the Armed Forces, who are, it is stressed, first and

[80] It is printed in Nogueira Filho, op. cit. *A Guerra Cívica* 1932. I. 381–94.

[81] *O indivíduo integral:* Nogueira Filho, op. cit. I. 389. *Integral* is an adjective which appears ever more frequently in Legionary writing. Salgado was, of course, the principal author of this manifesto.

[82] Torres's nationalist ideas were much in vogue at this time. For a recent comment on them, cf. Barbosa Lima Sobrinho, 'Alberto Torres, Sua Vida e Sua Obra', *Revista Civilizaçao Brasileira* (5–6 March 1966), 325–42.

[83] '. . . Our word of command must be *brasilidade*. . . . The 1891 constitution was the cause of all the evils of the Republic . . . precisely because it was made *for* Brazil and not *by* Brazil. . . .' Nogueira Filho, op. cit., I. 387–8.

foremost *Brazilians* and whose co-operation with the Legion is especially requested.

These, then, are some of the main ideas behind the Legion and the National Revolutionary Party. The archives contain other schemes and plans, some of which are directly linked to the Legion, and others which are less easy to place. The first group includes, for instance, a scheme, signed by Frederico Cristiano Buys, dated 22 January 1931, headed *Bases for a Unified Plan of Promotions, and other related Regulations, for Officers of the Army and Navy and for Civil Servants*, which discussed many long-standing grievances felt, especially by junior officers.[84] Another in the same file, entitled *Legion of October. Section for Education and Indoctrination*, proposes elaborate regulations, including, for instance, a financial obligation on employers to contribute to the education of their employees in a fight against illiteracy.

In the second group there is an interesting manifesto announcing the *Partido Regenerador Paulista*, dated São Paulo, 1 February 1931,[85] emphasizing the *município* as the basic unit of political organization, and another, in the same file, laying down principles for founding a Radical Nationalist Party. Most interesting of all is a long, detailed manifesto of the Brazilian Nationalist Party (*Partido Nacionalista Brasileiro*,[86] again aiming to replace existing parties and with explicit praise for Mussolini. Though coinciding in many respects with the programmes of the Legion and P.R.N., it gives more attention to social and labour policies. *Section C*, for example, demands a maximum working day of eight hours (seven for night shifts), and a minimum weekly rest of thirty-six consecutive hours. It prescribes payment in legal currency, the fixing of minimum wages by mixed committees of workers and employers, and better working conditions for both urban and rural workers. *Section D* provides for a national insurance scheme against unemployment, sickness, accident at work, old age and death, and for maternity benefits. *Section F* (Education) demands priority application of public funds for primary education, with free, lay and obligatory education for all children under fifteen. These are also to be given free books and, where necessary, free meals and clothing. Night classes, again free, are to be set up for adults, including technical instruction, and there is to be a reform of secondary and university education, again to be made free to the most able candidates.

[84] *Aranha Papers*, F.32, Ministério da Justiça.
[85] *Aranha Papers*, F.42, Ministério de Justiça.
[86] *Aranha Papers*, F.42, Ministério da Justiça.

The origins of many of these schemes are not clear, and it seems that they are often parallel, complementary developments to that of the Legion and the P.R.N. They all reflect, however, the general confusion of the period and they show that, while the Liberal Alliance itself may not have produced detailed plans for revolutionary government, the revolution soon stimulated all kinds of programmes and projects. But all of them, at this stage, were ideas only on paper. One now needs to examine how, if at all, in the case of the Legion, the ideas were applied and the reaction they produced.

IV. *The reaction*

Frederico Cristiano Buys was right in his forecast that the real test of the Legion would come in São Paulo, Minas Gerias, and Rio Grande do Sul, where it must meet the strongly established state political organizations. Nowhere was reaction more intense than in São Paulo and the history of the Legion in São Paulo is a large part of the story of the 1932 Paulista revolt. As such, it cannot be examined in detail here; but it is enough to see why, in general terms, it failed— why, indeed, it was already bound to fail even before the publication of its manifesto in March 1932.

In São Paulo, the Legion became entangled, right from the start, in the struggle for political control between the civilian politicians of the Democratic party and the predominantly tenente group, led by João Alberto Lins de Barros and, increasingly, by Miguel Costa, the tenente leader so prominent in the march of the "Miguel Costa-Prestes Column' from 1925–7. The death of Siqueira Campos had removed the leader of the revolution in São Paulo, and the struggle for power began even before the revolution was won. The Democrats firmly believed that they would provide the new state government,[87] but the tenentes and some of the more radical politicians were suspicious of their Democratic allies, whom they regarded as, essentially, no different from the São Paulo Republican party, the P.R.P.[88] They especially disagreed with the Democrats' emphasis on electoral reform as the primary remedy for Brazil's problems and they distrusted the Democrats' tendency, despite the national organization of their party, to appeal to narrow Paulista pride and interests. Though Vargas tried to reach agreement on who should govern São Paulo, it became clear within twenty-four hours of his arrival in the city en

[87] Nogueira Filho, op. cit. II. 568, 583. V. Mello Franco, op. cit., p. 373.

[88] Cf. Buys, p. 83 above. Also, for a similar comment: U.S. State Department: 832.00/695. Cameron (S. Paulo) 18 Nov. 1930.

route to the federal capital that no consensus was possible.[89] Eventually, João Alberto was appointed on Aranha's insistence,[90] with General Isidoro Dias Lopes remaining as commander of the second Military Division.

Unfortunately, João Alberto's appointment, so contrary to the Democrats' expectations, caused intense and bitter resentment in São Paulo. His arbitrary behaviour especially antagonized employers and industrialists,[91] and, together with his apparent tolerance of communists in São Paulo,[92] laid him open to charges of irresponsibly cultivating the workers' support, with the Legion regarded as one of his primary means. The very fact that his signature was on the announcement of the Legion on the 12 November was enough to condemn it at once as far as many Paulistas were concerned. Though João Alberto could write to Vargas on 20 November that the Legion was 'having much

[89] Vargas arrived in São Paulo on 28 October. On 24 October the military junta had asked Francisco Morato to take over the Paulista government, but he had refused until he could consult Vargas. For these difficulties, see Leven Vampré, *São Paulo, terra conquistada* (S. Paulo, 1932), pp. 48–9. Nogueira Filho, op. cit. II. 565. V. Mello Franco, op. cit., pp. 376–7. During discussions in the Campos Elísios palace on the 28 and 29, it became clear that Morato was unacceptable to most of the revolutionary leaders and that the Democrats themselves were divided. It was therefore decided that São Paulo should, for the present, be governed by a secretariat made up exclusively of Paulista civilians, with João Alberto acting as the revolution's military delegate in São Paulo. Paulo Nogueira Filho claims that the issue was decided before ever Vargas reached São Paulo, since Aranha, Góes Monteiro, and others of the 'Grupo de Comando' were, he says, determined not to risk losing control of the revolution, not even to Miguel Costa: Filho, op. cit. II. 556.

[90] Cf. Aranha to Vargas, 21 Nov. 1930—*Vargas Papers*, Nov. 1930, p. 19: 'I insist, with the perseverance of friendship, on João's nomination. . . . I feel bad about insisting, but I cannot adopt any other attitude, granted my knowledge of the situation'. The day before, 20 Nov. 1930, João Alberto himself wrote to Vargas urging the need to appoint an interventor and end the role of the politicians: ibid., p. 17. According to João Neves, Vargas said that, despite Aranha's insistence, he would not appoint João Alberto: J. Neves, *Accuso!* (Rio de Janeiro, 1933), p. 22.

[91] On 17 November, for instance, by which time strikes in São Paulo were affecting nearly ten thousand workmen, the press published a decree, on João Alberto's authority, ordering, among other things, that workers' wages should be raised by 5 per cent and that employers should provide at least 40 hours' work per week. It also announced the formation, by 30 November, of a Commission of Labour Legislation, with representation for workmen who should be of age and Brazilian by birth. In fairness to João Alberto, it should be noted that he had already appointed a committee of Democrats to discuss the labour problem, but it had proved ineffective.

[92] Nogueira Filho, op. cit. II. 587.

success here' and that he was only awaiting the arrival of Aranha to work out details of its programme,[93] his close personal association with it caused many to reject the Legion out of hand as the personal instrument of João Alberto and Miguel Costa in the humiliation of São Paulo.[94]

By the time the Libertador leader, Assis Brasil, arrived in São Paulo on 17 November, he found himself the centre of a sharp struggle between the Democrats and the new Legionaries.[95] Relations between the two groups then worsened over the next two weeks, culminating in the crisis of 3 December, when the São Paulo state government resigned in protest against João Alberto's government and the growing power of the Legion.[96] The Democrats and their supporters continued to protest strongly to Vargas about the arbitrary behaviour of João Alberto and the 'military' led by Costa. On 24 November, José María Whitaker passed on to Vargas a letter from Plínio Barreto, on the growing disillusion of loyal supporters of the revolution who now, rightly or wrongly, think 'that we are being condemned to a military dictatorship of a Communist nature'.[97] On 7 December, Paulo de Moraes Barros expressed similar alarm.

Such fears seemed justified by the steady growth of the Legion in São Paulo. By January 1931 Miguel Costa reported that the Legion was now organized in every district of the state,[98] and reports put the

[93] *Vargas Papers.* November 1930, p. 17.
[94] So Nogueira Filho, op. cit. II. 594, seeing it as directed against the Democrats. For a similar reaction, both reporting and reflecting local feeling, cf. Morgan's report of 20 Nov. 1930: '. . . it is not improbable that the real object of its [the Legion's] formation is to support João Alberto, the carpet-bag temporary administrator of the state of São Paulo, who by his adoption of a radical labor policy has alienated the sentiments of . . . the better classes in that town and state. . . .' *U.S. State Dept.* 820.00/689.
[95] The Legion, with an announcement in the press of 17 November, signed 'Pedroso', claimed that they alone, as the most genuine revolutionaries, should meet Assis Brasil, a challenge which the Democrats at once took up. A crowd of about 200,000 met Assis Brasil, with the Democratic party taking the lead: see *Estado de São Paulo,* 18 Nov. 1930.
[96] The Paulistas' resentment was clearly expressed in an article by J. E. de Macedo Soares in *Diário Nacional* of 6 December. He speaks bitterly of the power of men 'who are not even Paulistas'. São Paulo, he says, is faced with a 'Military Soviet'.
[97] Whitaker had already written to Vargas on 21 November, suggesting that either Assis Brasil or João Neves should take over in São Paulo. *Vargas Papers.* Oct.–Dec. 1930, p. 18. For Costa, see the letter of Paulo de Moraes Barros, ibid., Oct.–Dec. 1930, p. 31.
[98] To Marrey Junior, *Aranha Papers,* F.22, Ministério de Justiça.

Legion's strength at about seventeen thousand,[99] its growth being helped by the split in the Democratic party with greater control going to its more conservative members.[1]

The Legion's apparent strength, however, was really deceptive. Already it was having difficulties other than opposition from the Democrats. By the turn of the year João Alberto, spending more time cultivating the *fazendeiro* party,[2] found it harder to agree with all the Legion's ideas, especially on coffee,[3] and there were widespread rumours of a split between him and Miguel Costa and, still more, between them both and the commander of the Second Military District, General Isidoro Dias Lopes. By March 1931, when the São Paulo Legion issued its manifesto, Isidoro strongly distrusted and disliked the pretensions of the Legion. People were eager, therefore, to see his reaction to the manifesto of the São Paulo Legion when it appeared on 4 March.

The manifesto received scant welcome in São Paulo. It was attacked by the Chateaubriand press and, of course, by the Democrats' *Diário Nacional*.[4] Only the *Estado de São Paulo* was at first non-committal; even those papers usually regarded as expressing the views of João Alberto (the *Folha da Tarde* and the *Folha da Manha*) were hostile to the manifesto. Observers were quick to notice that João Alberto, despite his part in launching the Legion the previous November, did not sign the manifesto. General Isidoro was asked for his views in a press interview, and was surprisingly mild in his comments. The General, however, was only trying to be loyal to the revolution, and letters which he wrote to Vargas show how far he had been alienated by the activities of the Legion.[5] On 9 April he wrote offering his resignation, giving as his main reason his inability to accept the

[99] U.S. State Dept., 832.00/17—Cameron (S. Paulo) 7 Mar. 1931. This was probably an exaggeration as Cameron himself noted, but recruitment certain was heavy.

[1] See Cameron, ibid., 832.00/711—S. Paulo, 13 Feb. 1931 [the Democratic party] 'is now the most conservative party in São Paulo. . . .'

[2] See his address of 19 Jan. 1931 to the *Sociedade Rural Brasileira*, demanding that 'São Paulo should be directed by those who produce.'

[3] See his letter to Vargas (*Vargas Papers*, Oct.–Nov. 1930, p. 54) demanding help for the São Paulo coffee growers, since the salvation or ruin of the whole country depends on this.

[4] See Nelson Tabajara de Oliveira in *Diário Nacional* of 6 March.

[5] Isidoro had already written to Vargas at the end of January, describing his lack of sympathy with João Alberto and Miguel Costa, and offering to resign his military command. *Vargas Papers*, Jan.–July 1931, 29 Jan. 1931.

behaviour of João Alberto and Miguel Costa, who, also, he believed, must leave São Paulo if peace was to be preserved:

'... what is being done here is both wrong and criminal. ... I am told that all is to remain as it is in São Paulo and that Dr. Oswaldo Aranha, justifying this preservation of the *status quo* in São Paulo, told Dr. Júlio de Mesquita that sixty *tenentes*, not agreeing with the departure of Colonel João Alberto, had declared they would come here, fully armed, to resist such a solution ... if even Dr. Oswaldo Aranha regards himself as a prisoner of the *tenentes*, what of myself who am not *persona grata* with these Neo-revolutionaries?[6]

Others, too, bitterly attacked the Legion. On 20 March 1931, Luís Carlos Prestes sent from Buenos Aires a manifesto to *Diário da Noite* of São Paulo:[7]

'Aranha, Collor, Miguel Costa, Távora, with their cynical assistants Motta Lima, Raphael Correa, Reis Perdigão, and many others, from north to south, are organizing Revolutionary Legions, engaging in the most barefaced demagoguery. ...'

Their aim, Prestes alleged, was to lead soldiers and sailors to new bloodshed, in fights between Isidoro and Miguel Costa, between João Alberto and the Democrats. The Legion, it seemed, was under fire from every side.

Prestes at least was right in seeing bitter struggles ahead. Indeed, already in São Paulo such struggles were descending to the municipal level. On 7 April, for example, the *prefeito* of São Luís de Parahytingá wrote to the Ministry of Justice, complaining that Democratic party supporters there, who supported the October revolution, were now being persecuted by members of Miguel Costa's Revolutionary Legion.[8] Many of these new Legionaries had been *perrepistas*,[9] he said, and under their local leader they were now doing everything possible to harass loyal revolutionary Democrats. On 22 June, Oswaldo Aranha's uncle wrote a similar letter from Jundiahy, São Paulo,

---

[6] *Vargas Papers*, Jan.–July 1931. In another letter to a naval officer (the name of the addressee has been torn), dated 9 April, Isidoro speaks even more bitterly of pretentious young revolutionaries with no respect for democracy and of the *Força Pública* and the *Revolutionary Legion* '... equipped and armed to the teeth, organized by the Interventor, by General Miguel and Colonel Mendonça Lima ...'— *Aranha Papers*, F.22, 6 Apr. 1931.

[7] *Vargas Papers*, Jan.–July 1931, p. 29.

[8] *Aranha Papers*, F.23, Ministério da Justiça.

[9] Viz. members of the P.R.P., São Paulo Republican Party.

regretting that the Legion had not lived up to its original ideas.[10] The Legion, he pointed out, was now the only channel of political patronage in the interior, 'the only channel by which one can reach government departments. . .'. Unfortunately, the Legion had been taken over by irresponsible elements.

There are other complaints of the same kind.[11] All show, unmistakably, that by the middle of 1931 the Legion in São Paulo had failed in its primary purpose. Instead of creating a new revolutionary party capable of transcending narrow state rivalries and interests, it had, in fact, become inextricably entangled in the political squabbles of the state. It was irreconcilably at odds with all the most powerful political groups, with the Democratic party, with the Republicans, with General Isidoro and many in the federal garrison, with the industrialists and bankers and the most important of the coffee interests. Although still powerful and, indeed, still growing stronger, its appeal was, essentially, to the workers of São Paulo, hoping for a new deal from the revolution.

In July 1931 came its most dramatic test of strength, when Miguel Costa and the Legion were able, against intense opposition, to prevent Plínio Barreto from succeeding João Alberto at the head of the São Paulo government.[12] Though clearly revealing the Legion's power, the victory was a Pyrrhic one. Barreto was excluded and the Democrats humiliated, but the last hope had gone of any reconciliation in São Paulo between the Legion and the other political groupings in the state.

In the next twelve months, Miguel Costa and the Legion played an important part in pushing São Paulo towards revolt. The Legion grew in strength[13] and Costa tried, unsuccessfully, to turn it into an acceptable political party, the São Paulo Popular party, but the very attempt showed how far the Legion had abandoned its original ambitions. When violence finally broke out in São Paulo on 23 May

[10] Ibid.

[11] Ibid., F.22.

[12] Maurício Goulart, the secretary general of the Legion in São Paulo, stated their position clearly in a telegram to Vargas of 15 July 1931: 'Urgent. The Revolutionary Legion . . . begs to inform you that it considers the nomination of Plínio Barreto a victory for the Democratic Party . . . prejudicial to the peace desired by the Paulista people. . . .' *Aranha Papers*, F.32.

[13] In a long letter to Aranha of 3 Oct. 1931, describing his efforts to turn the Legion into a political party, Costa said that the congress of the Legion the previous month had represented over 500 *distritos de paz* and over 300,000 enrolled Legionaries.

1932, the offices of the Legion were among the first to be attacked
and Costa and his supporters were among the first targets of the
Paulistas when the revolt started in July. By its immediate, inesacapable
embroilment in local political controversies, the Legion, designed to
end such quarrels, finished, ironically, in São Paulo by ruining any
hopes of a settlement in Brazil's most important state and by leading,
as a major cause to the most serious political crisis of the 1930s.

In Rio Grande do Sul, the Legion was never as powerful as in
São Paulo, but the strong reaction, even to the suggestion of organizing
it, again reveals the opposition to any notion of supra-state revolutionary party. There were gauchos who welcomed the idea of the
Legion,[14] but mostly it provoked suspicion and rumours of military
plots and of aims to destroy the existing gaucho political parties.[15] On
23 March 1931, Aranha's own brother, Luís, wrote to him from Rio
Grande do Sul, reporting that the Legion could not survive in the south:

'I cannot deny that the bulk of public opinion in Rio Grande is hostile to the
Legion. You yourself know better than anyone the intensity of party feeling
here, as a result of the struggles of the past. . . . Consequently, the Legion
cannot be warmly received. . . . For the gauchos the death of these parties is the
death of Rio Grande itself. . . . You know this from your own experience. . . .'

On 31 March, the same issues were taken up in a long, important
letter to Aranha from Borges de Medeiros.[17] Borges refers to the
'sinister spectre of militarism', the threat of a military coup, which
he sees as an imminent danger. It was to oppose this threat, he says,
that Aranha thought of creating the Legion of October which,
according to the scheme given to Borges by Dr. Raul Bittencourt
and the recent statements to the press of Minister Francisco Campos,
has all the characteristics of a 'civilian militia' and a 'political organization'. Both of these aspects of the Legion alarm Borges, so he suggests
what he thinks may be an acceptable alternative:

'From the political point of view, what seems to me preferable is the organization of a strong national party. . . . I always hoped, as was logical, that the
Liberal Alliance might be transformed into such a party. . . .'[18]

[14] See Caío Pedro Moacyr to Aranha 11 Mar. 1931. *Aranha Papers*, F.22.
[15] *Aranha Papers*, F.23, Min. Justiça. Also see the report of José Leite de Oliveira
of 12 Oct. 1931, ibid. As when, on 3 April 1931, Heitor da Fontoura Rangel wrote
from Porto Alegre to Captain Alcides Etchegoyen, complaining bitterly of
rumours of military government in Rio Grande do Sul, and of Vargas's failure
to carry out the aims of the Liberal Alliance.   [16] Ibid.   [17] Ibid.
[18] This, of course, coincided exactly with what Aranha and the Legionaries had

What concerns Borges, however, is how the Legions, now established, can be reconciled with the autonomous existence of the parties already in Rio Grande do Sul, 'none of which wishes to die or repudiate its traditions or programme or its free organization'. Borges, therefore, suggests his alternative scheme:

'Granted the circumstances, I see no other way out but the founding of a league or federation of parties and Legions, with one *centralised executive*, one *common programme* and one code of rules. This League or federation could be called the *National Union* (União Nacional), or take whatever name best characterises it. It should, however, be absolutely clear that the component members . . . will continue to rule themselves freely by their own local statutes in matters pertaining only to the state. . . . In this way only can we safeguard the federative principle which none of us is willing to sacrifice. . . .'

The constitution of this new Union, Borges then suggests, should be decided at a conference in Porto Alegre.

Despite the friendly tone of this letter—with love from Borges and Carlinda to Oswaldo and D. Vidinha—it was, of course, a clear note of warning not to meddle in Rio Grande.[19] A watered-down version of the Legion, capable of being further weakened in long committee discussions, and leaving the existing parties intact, was acceptable: nothing more. Aranha, if still a loyal member of the Rio Grande Republican party, must heed the warning from the undisputed political chefe of Rio Grande.

This was the authentic voice of the state, expressing the general gaucho reaction, described in another letter to Aranha from his old friend, Fausto de Freitas e Castro, written in Porto Alegre, 30 May 1931.[20] He bitterly reproaches the provisional government for failing to stand by the promises of the Liberal Alliance, for dissolving state assemblies and for failing to govern according to the constitution, so behaving just as had the government of Washington Luís. Why was

---

been saying. There is little evidence that Borges had hoped to turn the Liberal Alliance into a national party: quite the contrary, though he does repeat this statement in an article in *A Federação* of 9 April 1931.

[19] It is interesting to compare this letter with a much more bitter one sent by Borges to Vargas, 10 Apr. 1931. *Vargas Papers*, Jan.–July 1931, p. 48. There the complaints are much stronger. They are also stronger in interviews given at the time by Raul Pilla, vice-president of the Libertador party, as in that of 4 March 1931, printed in the *Estado de São Paulo* of 5 March.

[20] *Aranha Papers*, F.23, Ministério da Justiça.

there still no return to constitutional rule? Above all, how could Aranha countenance the behaviour of Francisco Campos and the Legion in Minas?

'The manifesto launched by that Minister is appalling, unworthy of a man of his intelligence and culture. And he makes himself totally ridiculous, dressed in his khaki shirt and making empty, sonorous speeches. . . .'

The Legion's campaign in Minas, says Freitas e Castro, is directed entirely against the P.R.M. (Minas Republican Party). It is based on Campos's personal, political ambition. It is contrary to the whole constitutional spirit of the October revolution. This, he adds, was certainly not Aranha's idea when he launched the Legion, seeking to form a sort of United Front from north to south of Brazil to sustain and carry out the ideals of the revolution.

The relevance of these remarks to Minas can be seen later. Much more important was the outcry against the failure to return swiftly to constitutional rule and the apparent abandonment of the ideals of the Liberal Alliance. This was the cry which was to grow louder over the coming months until, finally, Vargas and Aranha were left isolated with the resignation from the provisional government of the other gaucho leaders, Neves, Luzardo, Collor and Cardoso on, ostensibly, this very issue. Borges, too, turned against them, leading an abortive revolt in conjunction with the Paulistas, so that only the loyalty of Flores da Cunha and his state forces prevented Rio Grande from joining São Paulo in destroying the Vargas government.

In other states, too, the reaction, though less intense and less important, was very similar. On 30 March 1931 Aranha wired to Captain Barata, Interventor of Pará, telling him 'the idea of the Legion grows daily into an irresistible force' and urging him to take on its organization in Pará.[21] One thing perhaps he had in mind was a series of letters which he had received from Annapolis, reporting enthusiasm for the Legion in Goiás, presenting the Legion as providing the disciplined revolutionary force needed to transform political life in the interior.[22] He was also hearing, at the same time, a report of the swift growth of the Legion in Santa Catharina, and its influence as against that of the *Partido Liberal*.[23] Unfortunately, the very first of these letters reveals the immediate submersion of the Legion into the old pattern

[21] *Aranha Papers*, F.32, Min. Justiça.
[22] See letters from Victor Coelho de Almeida to Aranha, 4 Mar. 1931–21 Mar. 1931, ibid.
[23] Letter of Henrique Rupp Junior, 5 Mar. 1931, *Aranha Papers*, F.23.

of state politics. The state, it points out, has been dominated politically by the Ramos family.[24] There have been so many branches (*ramos*) from this particular trunk that they have provided shelter for all kinds of political animals. But now there is at last a means of fighting this *caciquismo ramosta*. 'The Revolutionary Legion. This will be my party.' On 20 April, Rupp Júnior, President of the newly formed Santa Catharina Legion, sent another revealing report: he estimates that within two months it will have over sixty thousand members, such is the enthusiasm locally. Two tenentes, however, have, he says, Communist tendencies and are working for Dr. Nereu Ramos to subvert the Legion. Then follows a bitter denunciation of Ramos, who has gone to Rio de Janeiro to try to resist the Legion's growth or, at least, to get named as official representative to the Santa Catharina Legion one of Ramos's own men or one of the 'Communist' tenentes. The whole letter, stuffed with its bogus figures and bitter, petty, local rancour, could hardly have cheered Aranha, but it is an excellent example of how, universally, the Legion was at once absorbed into the old pattern of local politics.[25]

Much more encouraging was the manifesto of the Legion of October of the State of Rio de Janeiro (*Legião de Outubro Fluminense*) dated 6 April 1931. This is a much tougher, crisper document, beginning with general statements of principle, then proceeding to detailed, specific objectives.[26] It appealed to all classes and groups and started with a severe denunciation of the unrepresentative nature of politics in the Republic since 1889. Learning the lessons of the past, the new Republic must not follow foreign models, whatever their character, but seek a political system suited to Brazil, with representation suited to the size and degree of development of the country. The Legion, said the manifesto, favoured indirect suffrage, with a secret, obligatory vote for all men and women over eighteen years old. Then it descended to specific objectives: under Agriculture, it proposed a national register of all landholdings, a break-up of *latifundio*, creation of agricultural colleges in all the leading states, the founding of a *Banco de Crédito Agrícola* to help smaller farmers, an increase in workers' co-operatives

[24] So in the congress for organizing the Liberal party in the state: 'Foi eleito presidente honorario—Vidal Ramos. Leader do partido—Ramos. Secretario do Estado—Ramos. Juíz Federal—Ramos.'

[25] On 5 September 1931, Rupp Júnior announced the transformation of the Legion in S. Catharina into a new political party, the *Legião Republicana Catarinense*, and enclosed its programme and statutes. *Aranha Papers*, F.23, Min. Justiça.

[26] *Aranha Papers*, F.23, Min. Justiça.

G

and regular congresses of workers to discuss their immediate interests. A section on Instruction and Education demanded reforms and improvements at every level, from nursery schools to university reform and technical and industrial training. An important set of demands covered Social Services and Health, proposing new hospitals, free medicine and serious attention to the health and welfare of all Brazilians. The section, Labour and Capital, demanded improved working conditions, workers' insurance, a minimum wage related to the cost of living, statutory holidays and the construction of workers' houses and 'garden suburbs'.

This manifesto from the Legion in the state of Rio de Janeiro is one of the clearest, most concise and progressive programmes to come out of the 1930 revolution. It proposes sensible solutions to real problems without at any time underestimating the difficulties involved. Unfortunately, the Fluminense Legion, like all the others, was to have only a very short existence before being discredited by the more dramatic political failures of the Legions in São Paulo and Minas Gerais.[27]

Other states, too, produced their Legions and programmes, and it was the São Paulo Legion and the Legion of Minas Gerais which provided the models for those of the other states. It was the Legion in Minas Gerais which brought the whole Legionary experiment into disrepute and, ultimately, to failure.

The Legion in Minas, right from the start, took on a notably different character from that of São Paulo. Partly the difference sprang from the characters of the men who directed it, the Minas manifesto of 26 February 1931 being signed by Francisco Campos, minister of Education, Gustavo Capanema, secretary of the Interior in Minas, and Amaro Lanari, Minas secretary of Finance.[29] The manifesto, shorter than that of São Paulo, which soon followed it, consisted mainly of vague aims,

[27] Another interesting document from the Estado do Rio, partly complementary to, partly, it seems, a reaction to the Legion, is the *Proclamation to the Army* from the Revolutionary Committee of the State of Rio, dated April 1931 and now in the *Vargas Papers* (Vol. 2, Jan.–July, 1931, p. 39). It violently attacks the political parties in Minas and Rio Grande, then sets out a programme which, again, urges the need to *abrasileirisar o Brasil*. Under headings of O *Problema Militar*, O *Problema Político*, and O *Problema Económico Social*, it presents a long detailed programme, in many ways similar to that of the Fluminense Legion, but it ends with a severe attack on the 'fascism of the Legions', especially in Minas. I have so far been unable to find out much about this 'Revolutionary Committee'.

[28] *Aranha Papers*, F.23, Min. Justiça: for Paraná see Report dated 7 May 1931 from Curitiba; for Maranhão letter of 22 October 1931 from São Luíz.

[29] The manifesto appeared in the press of 27 February.

such as to defend the revolution and realize its ideals, opposing its enemies wherever they came from. One particular characteristic of the Minas Legion, reflecting the interests of Campos, was the special loyalty it proclaimed to the Catholic Church, especially in the matter of religious education, an issue which at once aroused controversy. More conspicuous still were the external trappings of the Minas Legionaries, with their khaki shirts (the shirt of the soldier and worker), and the flags and banners of European-style Fascism. There was much less emphasis on brasilidade in the Minas Legion and a much closer following of European, especially Italian, Fascism. Partly, too, the difference between the São Paulo and Minas Legions reflected the difference in the two states. The Paulista Legion had to set itself to appeal, in large part, to urban workers in an increasingly industrial milieu, hence its close attention to economic and social issues, whereas the Minas Legion, appearing in a much more rigidly conservative state, was never designed to appeal to, but rather to be imposed on, the people. Whatever its faults, the Paulista Legion envisaged reconstruction, looking to the future, whereas the Legion in Minas was still concerned, essentially, with the local political quarrels of the Old Republic.[30] But it is the close modelling of itself on European movements which most distinguishes the Minas Legion and it was this element which, in later years, was its most conspicuous contribution to Brazilian *Integralismo*, joining the panoply of European Fascism to Salgado's ideas of brasilidade. It is, on the other hand, a mistake to let the differences between the two Legions obscure their common origins in the desire of Aranha, Campos, other politicians and tenentes, to create a new revolutionary force with the Legion, just as they tried, too, with the 3rd October Club. The distinctions must not be drawn too sharply.

The criticism of the Minas Legion by Fausto de Freitas e Castro has already been quoted. Similar scorn was expressed in many other letters and telegrams to Vargas and Aranha, as, for instance, in a series of letters to Aranha from Belo Horizonte, in April 1931, signed

[30] An interesting comparison of the two Legions, which makes this last point, can be found in a long report sent to Aranha on 6 March 1931 by Salles Filho— *Aranha Papers*, F.23, Min. Justiça. Aranha, on 5 March, had asked Salles Filho to compare the manifestos of the two Legions to see if they could be reconciled in the programme of the *Legião Carioca*, which he was then drawing up. Salles Filho thinks they are irreconcilable, since the Minas Legion is essentially conservative and incapable of being transformed into a *national* party of the revolution. Salles Filho thinks the Legion can be different from state to state, but must always have this quality.

'Maximiliano'.[31] There is nothing but scorn for the Minas Legion, described as 'the bastard child of a good idea' and ridicule for Campos's boasting about 'Legionary forces which exist only in his imagination'. There is urgent need for federal intervention in Minas Gerais.

This, however, was precisely one of the difficulties in the Minas situation, namely that, because of the co-operation of the state president, Olegário Maciel, in the October revolution, Minas Gerais was the only state to be left without an interventor, remaining, instead, under its previous governor. Worse still, the two rival parties left in Minas after the revolution, namely the new Legion, created by Campos and supporting Maciel, and the old *P.R.M.* (*Partido Republicano Mineiro*), led by the former state and federal president, Artur Bernardes, could both claim to have supported Vargas in October 1931.[32] This meant that both groups now looked to Vargas for the rewards of office and patronage which they might expect under the coronelismo system,[33] and it was in this context of political rivalry, frustration, and recrimination, that the Legion in Minas began to grow.

Involvement in the tortuous, intensely personal controversy of state politics could hardly have been greater, again ruining any hopes of making the Legion a supra-state party as Aranha had originally wished. What, however, is particularly interesting in the Minas case, as an illustration of *how* the Legion became so involved, is that much of this controversy is reflected in reports and complaints made at the time to Vargas and to Aranha as Minister of Justice.

Already on 8 November 1930 Flores da Cunha wrote to Aranha that trouble was brewing in Minas and the Republicans were dissatisfied.[34] The government tried to remove one cause of the problem by offering Artur Bernardes the embassy in Paris. His refusal was

[31] See especially 27 Apr. 1931. *Aranha Papers* F.23, Min. da Justiça. I have been unable to identify 'Maximiliano'.

[32] The P.R.M. had, of course, broken with normal Brazilian practice by refusing to follow the lead of the federal president, Washington Luís, in the question of the presidential succession in 1930, supporting, instead, the Liberal Alliance. The Legion equally claimed to represent the revolution of October to be, indeed, its finest expression. The only Minas group to support Washington Luís had been a dissident group of the P.R.M., the *Concentração Conservadora*, led by Washington Luís's Vice-president, Carvalho Britto. This group had primarily broken with the P.R.M. over who was to succeed António Carlos as state president in 1930, so creating bitterness which was to persist after October 1930.

[33] How this system worked is clearly explained in the study by Victor Nunes Leal, already quoted. The political crisis in Minas after October 1930, the 'caso Mineiro', was largely the result of this breakdown in the coronelismo system.

[34] *Aranha Papers*, F.15, Correspondência Recda.

widely interpreted as an act of defiance, so much so that Bernardes felt obliged to write to Vargas on 11 February denying rumours that he was conspiring against him.[35] In March and April the situation grew worse as the Legionaries, perhaps emboldened by Vargas's apparent support,[36] became increasingly aggressive towards members of the Republican party and anyone who would not join their ranks.[37] From May onwards, complaints from the municípios of Minas reached the Ministry of Justice and the president's office almost daily.

The first seems to have come from Belo Horizonte on 28 May,[38] signed by five Republicans; the letter complains of persecution of Republicans throughout the state. Campos and the Legion are trying to force prefeitos to join the Legion, and those who do not lose their jobs. They are also using a Legionary militia in Belo Horizonte and elsewhere to suppress any kind of propaganda or demonstration in favour of the Republican party, and are using state funds illegally, not only to bring Legionaries by train to Belo Horizonte, but even to buy khaki shirts and other equipment for the Legionary militia.

Campos did, in fact, seem determined to destroy the Republican party.[39] On 2 June, Jayme Pinheiro, a former state deputy, protested to Vargas from Oliveira, over the Legion's dismissal of the prefeito and others because they were not Legionaries,[40] and on 11 June the deposed prefeito wrote at length to Aranha giving all the details.[41] He had been head of the *Junta Revolucionária* in the município and had worked hard for the revolution, but now he and other loyal revolutionaries were replaced by former supporters of Carvalho Britto and the *Concentração Conservadora*, all on the orders of Campos and Capanema. On 12 June two fazendeiros, Jovina Moreira Oliveira and Ilydio Mendes Magalhães, wired to Vargas that they had been imprisoned for five days in the município of Abre Campo and severely

[35] *Vargas Papers*, Vol. 2, Jan.–July 1931, p. 15.
[36] Cf. Vargas's comments on the Legion in *Correio da Manha*, reprinted *Diário Nacional* 18 Mar. 1931. Cf. Nogueira Filho, *A Guerra Cívica*, p. 50. Vargas was later less kind in his comments.
[37] *O Globo* of 17 April expressed the general concern over this, as did the *Estado de São Paulo* of the 18 noting the increasingly 'fascist' character of the Minas Legion, as in its proposed 'March on Belo Horizonte' scheduled for 21 April. Campos, in a speech on 4 April in the Teatro Central in Juíz de Fora, denied any intention of causing political divisions in the state.
[38] *Aranha Papers*, F.22, Min. da Justiça.
[39] Ibid., cf. Freitas e Castro to Aranha 30 May, F.23, Min. da Justiça.
[40] Ibid., F.22.
[41] *Aranha Papers*, F.23, Min. da Justiça.

beaten by the new Legionary authorities, who were imposing a regime of terror on the município.[42] On 18 June, Florentino Castellar Magalhães, ex-president of the chamber and of the Junta Revolucionária of Bambuhy, described to Vargas how all the local officials, including the postman, had been replaced by Legionaries, all of whom had supported Carvalho Britto and Washington Luís. The patience of the P.R.M. members is wearing thin, he says, and:

'. . . As the one who was responsible for the revolutionary movement in Bambuhy, where I kept two hundred men in arms . . . I wish to protest in the strongest fashion against . . . giving posts of responsibility to enemies of the nation and the revolution. . . .'[43]

Castellar Magalhães also wired to Vargas on 20 June, describing how Osório Maciel, Olégario's brother, was there to encourage the Legion, making life difficult for the P.R.M.[44] Similar complaints came from Manhuassú on 6 and 23 June,[45] and Montes Claros on 26.[46]

The Manhuassú case is worth looking at more carefully. On 6 June the Republicans in Manhuassú sent a long report to Vargas, who passed it on to the Ministry of Justice. The document is headed: *The Crimes . . . of the Legion of October in the Municipio of Manhuassú, Estado de Minas.* Manhuassú, it says, is one of the biggest, richest, and most productive municípios of the 'Zona de Matta' in Minas. In 1930 it supported Artur Bernardes, voted overwhelmingly for Getúlio Vargas, and worked for the revolution in Minas. But now it is being treated like an occupied enemy territory. Men are imprisoned and beaten up, homes are broken into, fazendas and *sítios* are attacked: no one is safe or protected by the law, and all for one reason only, that they are Bernardistas and Republicans. During the course of the last month, the report continues, Gustavo Capanema, as Secretary of the Interior for Minas, sent to the município a strong police force under the command of the 5th *Delegado Auxiliar* who declared in public that his job was 'to support the local Chief of the Legion . . . and get rid of the political friends of Sr. Artur Bernardes'. The report then describes the wave of persecution which followed, supplying names and details.

[42] Ibid.
[43] Ibid. He was obviously the local *coronel*, but two hundred men in arms must be an exaggeration.
[44] Ibid. Olégario himself is usually not blamed, following the old tradition of blaming his advisors. Campos, etc., are seen as taking advantage of Olégario's old age.
[45] *Aranha Papers*, F. 22.
[46] Ibid.

These include:

José Vieira Martins (*Director de Obras de Prefeitura*), imprisoned for a day and a night. Forced to leave the município under threats of violence. He was a leading supporter of Getúlio Vargas.

José Marau (carpenter), imprisoned for three days.

António Lopes (retired soldier), five days in prison. Beaten up in public. A loyal revolutionary.

Sebastião Silva (stonemason), three days in prison.

João Ferreira, José Ferreira, Miguel Ferreira (all farmworkers, sons of the fazendeiro Manoel Ferreira), two were imprisoned for three days, one for five. The last named was falsely accused of murder through witnesses who had been coerced.

Vincente Nolasco Estanislau (fazendeiro), arrested on his farm and taken to the city.

Agostinho da Costa Oliveira, arrested and beaten up.

José Salles Saab (merchant and coffee buyer, a man of high reputation), seized and brutally beaten up in the public gaol.

Adilio Cerqueira (fazendeiro, highly respected, belonging to an old, distinguished family in the município), because he was a Bernardista, his fazenda was surrounded and attacked by the police, who threatened to kill him, so that he has had to leave his family and his farm and take refuge outside the município.

Antonio da Silva Pedroso (fazendeiro in the district of Santa Helena), his farm was attacked at night and he was taken away and savagely beaten up.

One man, Estanislau de Salles, was even beaten up in daylight on the main street because he was wearing a tie which had on it a picture of Artur Bernardes. The report then analyses the leaders of the Legion in the município and, giving names and details, shows that in 1930, all of them were supporters of Júlio Prestes and the Concentração Conservadora.

Some of these complaints may, of course, be exaggerated, but the evidence is too dense and too consistent to leave any doubts about the wave of persecution and violence which the Legion brought to the municípios.[47] The Ministry of Justice files and the Vargas papers are full of such reports, coming from all over Minas—from Mutúm to

[47] Some, too, may seem extremely petty, but one should remember to see them in the Brazilian context, to understand, for instance, the humiliation and loss of face involved when a local fazendeiro or merchant of some standing was tossed into the common gaol and beaten up, especially when he had hoped for acknowledgement after October 1930.

Vargas on 3 July,[48] from Muriahé[49] and Cataguazes on 10.[50] In August they come even faster, culminating in the middle of the month in a crisis which even threatened the federal government and which lasted till the end of the year. This was the alleged, attempted *coup* by Bernardes against Maciel on the night of 17 August, following a congress of the *P.R.M.* in Belo Horizonte.[51] This, however, is a long, complicated story and the main point to establish here is how quickly the Legion in Minas, as everywhere else, became involved in local political struggles and how bitter was the reaction.

It was largely this reaction which caused Aranha, by October 1931, to withdraw his support for the Legion. He realized, not only from Minas, but also from São Paulo and, above all, from Rio Grande do Sul, that it was not really possible to impose a national reforming party on the whole of Brazil. He had, indeed, virtually disowned the Legion already in an interview to *Corréio do Povo* of Porto Alegre of 23 June 1931,[52] as he did again in a letter to Frederico Cristiano Buys of 21 September, answering some queries of Buys of 5 August.[53] Others, Buys among them, persisted in their attempts to build the Legion, but by July 1931 it had clearly moved away from its original ideals of providing a new, national revolutionary force to achieve the aims of the October revolution. It is not merely coincidence that efforts now begin in several states to turn the Legion into yet another local political party.

The swift, inevitable failure of the Legion should not, however, cause historians or even political scientists to ignore it. It did, after all, have some influence, particularly on the structure of the *Integralista* party, the most powerful civilian political grouping over the next few

[48] *Aranha Papers*, F.22, from Manoel Francisco again saying that Vargas's opponents are getting all the jobs.

[49] Ibid., signed 'Affonso Canedo'.

[50] Ibid., signed 'Pedro Dutra' and 'Armando Almeida'.

[51] This is a very detailed controversy. Some discussion of it can be found in Afonso Arinos de Melo Franco, *A Alma do Tempo* (Rio de Janeiro, 1961), which is criticized in Daniel de Carvalho, *Ensaios de Crítica e de História* (Rio de Janeiro, 1964). Both Vargas and Aranha were accused of trying to oust Maciel, and it is possible that Aranha, at least, was involved, hoping perhaps to push his candidate in Minas, Virgílio Melo Franco, as against Flores da Cunha's man, Gustavo Capanema. The story is all part of the contemporary concern to provide a successor to Vargas, whom, no one, of course, believed would govern Brazil for very much longer.

[52] See Nogueira Filho, op. cit., *A Guerra Cívica*, I. 169.

[53] *Aranha Papers*, F.23, Min. da Justiça. Recds.—Buys showed how bitterly he felt this break in a further letter to Aranha of 2 October, ibid.

years, which still leaves traces in Brazilian politics.[54] The Legion was, too, an important development within the revolution of October and, as such, cannot be neglected. Above all, its failure as a national political party is evidence of the nature of Brazilian politics in this and subsequent periods. The Legion is important as one of the first serious attempts at national political mobilization, to be followed later in the 1930s by equally abortive attempts with Integralismo and the A.N.L. But throughout the Old Republic the political system was such that the primary locus of power had been at the state level with the dominant political structures being those of the state political machines. Brazilian political culture was essentially state-oriented. The structural and cultural obstacles to national political organization through national parties were, and were to remain, insuperable. A national reforming party, based on a detailed programme, had no chance of success in that intensely personal, overwhelmingly local political system. The same, *mutatis mutandis*, could be said of later attempts to develop the Communist party, of Integralismo and of post-war national party organization. The only genuinely national group, the only vehicle, however inadequate, of national political mobilization was the army, which came, eventually, to fill the political vacuum.

Certainly, in 1931 a national revolutionary party had no function in terms of the political structures of Brazil. In this sense, therefore, perhaps the best epitaph for the Legion is a comment which its founder, Oswaldo Aranha, made much later on Integralismo, writing as ambassador to Washington on 10 February 1936:

'It will be a passing phenomenon, nothing more . . . obeying the Brazilian necessity to adapt itself to the land and people of the country'.[55]

---

[54] By November 1937, half the naval officers were said to support the Integralista movement. See *U.S. State Department* report of 6 November 1937, quoted by J. W. F. Dulles, *Vargas of Brazil: A Political Biography* (University of Texas Press, 1967), p. 166. This was certainly an exaggeration, but support undoubtedly was strong. It should also be remembered that Francisco Campos was the author of the *Estado Novo* constitution and, more recently, of the *1st Institutional Act* of 19 April 1964, following the *coup* of April 1964. A young mineiro protegé of his in the 1930s, who worked with Campos in 1936, when he was Secretary of Education in the Federal District, then again at the Ministry of Justice, was Carlos Medeiros Silva, himself Minister of Justice under Castello Branco and inspirer of the new constitution in January 1967.

[55] *Aranha Papers*, F.15, Correspondencia, Aranha to Martin Guilyan, 10 Feb. 1936.

LABOUR AND POLITICS IN CHILE*

by Alan Angell

ANY DISCUSSION of the political role of Chilean labour must examine the structure of the union movement, which, like most union movements, is the product of the structure of the economy, of legal regulation,[1] and of its political and social traditions. The emphasis of the paper is upon structure as well as ideas or attitudes, partly because ideas and attitudes are documented elsewhere,[2] partly because attitudes without structural analysis are less than revealing, and partly because this approach connects better with the political system. To make this connection relations with political parties are emphasized, because historically links between the political and economic activities of the labour movement have been strong, and because at the present time parties play an important role as brokers between the government and the unions, even if more frequently as bearers of declarations of war than of offers of peace. Both at the level of organization, through their *departmentos sindicales*, and at the level of theory, in their search for a doctrine of the appropriate role of the unions, the parties attempt to forge links with labour. Often the aims of their organizations and the

* The author wishes to acknowledge the generous help of the Royal Institute of International Affairs and of St. Antony's College, Oxford, in financing and supporting the project; and the hospitality of the *Instituto de Estudios Internacionales*, Santiago de Chile.

[1] The theory behind the legal framework was largely the result of the (unenlightened) paternalism of the Liberals and Conservatives in the early 1920s. For a detailed description of Conservative and Liberal ideas about labour legislation, see James Morris, *Elites, Intellectuals and Consensus* (New York, 1966).

[2] Notably in the publications of INSORA, Santiago de Chile; especially Manuel Barrera, *El Sindicato Industrial*, INSORA (1965); and Henry Landsberger, Manuel Barrera and Abel Toro, *El Pensamiento del Dirigente Sindical Chileno*, INSORA (1963). See also Torcuato di Tella, Lucien Brams, Jean Daniel Reynaud, and Alain Touraine, *Huachipato et Lota: Étude sur la conscience ouvrière dans deux entreprises chiliennes* (Paris, 1966).

ends of their theory have clashed; but more political creeds than
Marxism find it difficult to marry theory and practice.

SIZE, DISTRIBUTION, AND GROWTH OF THE LABOUR MOVEMENT

Obvious factors affecting the politics of any labour movement are
the size of the organized labour movement in relation to total labour
force, and its geographical and occupational distribution.

TABLE I

Total Public and Private Sector Labour Force in the Unions, 1966

Total Labour Force *minus*:		2,935,060
(a) age group 15–17 that cannot be union members	172,113	
(b) employers	39,239	
(c) armed forces and police	65,000	276,352
Total labour force that can form unions		2,658,708
Total labour force private sector in unions		314,795
Total labour force in public sector in 'associations'		215,781
		530,576 or 19·5% of total labour force.

Source: Ministry of Labour Figures, compiled by Clotario Blest and supplied
by the *Centro de Estudios Sindicales* of the University of Chile.

Of a labour force of nearly three million, about 10 per cent are
organized into unions recognized by the state. But if we add to this
total those state workers who have formed *gremios* or 'associations',
which in theory should not act like unions, but in practice do, then the
percentage in union-type organizations rises to nearly 20 per cent—
relatively high for Latin America. If we further excluded rural workers
and industrial workers in factories of 10 or less, the figure would be
much higher.

Unionized labour is concentrated in certain sectors of the economy.
Agriculture, in which 27 per cent of labour is employed, has a level
of unionization of only 3 per cent. But in this sector there have been
impressive changes since the Frei administration revised the law on the
formation of rural unions, and both numbers in unions and union
activity have started to rise dramatically.[3] There have always been

[3] Before 1947 rural workers could not form unions. The law was changed in
1947, but the conditions were so demanding that only a handful of unions were

certain agricultural occupations in which for special reasons (largely because the structure was 'industrial') illegal union activity was important, if sporadic. The vineyard workers of Molina[4] or the cattle-men of Magallanes are two examples.

The key mining industry, especially copper, employs only 4 per cent of the total labour force, but over half the mining workers are in unions. If we exclude those who work in small and medium-sized mining units, largely Chilean-owned in contrast to the largely American-owned *gran minería*, then the percentage of the labour force in unions is much higher.

In manufacturing industry about 27 per cent of the labour force is in unions, and the rate of unionization (and pay) increases more or less directly with the size of the undertaking.[5]

Geographically there is very considerable variation. The highest level of unionization is in Antofagasta, where 32 per cent of the labour force is organized, mostly in mining unions. In several rural provinces the level drops to 3 per cent or lower. In Santiago and its surroundings, where almost half of all unionists live and work, the proportion of the total labour force in unions is 12 per cent. Nearly 90 per cent of all unionists live in or near four major cities; Santiago, Valparaíso, Concepción and Antofagasta.[6]

Growth

The number of workers in unions, defined as paid up members of a permanent organization, is no necessary guide to the numbers which may be mobilized for specific industrial or political action. In the late nineteenth century there existed only a rudimentary organized labour movement, mostly mutualist societies, or resistance societies (largely Anarchist influenced and based in Valparaíso and Santiago), and

---

formed: Francisco Walker Linares, 'Trade Unionism among Agricultural Workers in Chile', *International Labour Review*, Vol. LXVIII, No. 6 (Geneva, 1953), pp. 509–23. But the Christian Democratic Government recently passed a law allowing for the formation of rural unions. (Text in *La Nación* (Santiago), 1 May 1967). See also James Petras, *Chilean Christian Democracy: Politics and Social Forces*. Politics of Modernization Series, No. 4 (Berkeley, California, 1967), Ch. 4, *passim*.

[4] A strike of vineyard workers in Molina in 1953 is analysed in Henry Landsberger and Fernando Canitrot, *Iglesia, Intelectuales y Campesinos* (Santiago, 1967).

[5] Jorge Barría, 'El Sistema de Relaciones Laborales en Chile', manuscript, INSORA (1966).

[6] The figures are those of the Ministry of Labour, as supplied by the *Centro de Estudios Sindicales* of the University of Chile.

brotherhoods (mostly in the northern mining areas). Nevertheless, far more than the theoretical membership could be mobilized for protest in times of crisis or hardship,[7] but this was more in the nature of spontaneous mass protest than planned union activity. Today the relationship between *formal* union membership and the number of workers who may be mobilized for strikes is much closer, but there are still variations between occupations; rural and mining to take the extreme examples.

Estimates of union membership are very speculative for the earlier period. Some estimates put the number in unions in 1903 as 63,000. By 1928, the first of the major trade union confederations, the *Federación Obrera de Chile* (FOCh), claimed to have organized some 136,000 workers.[8]

But reliable figures (for legal unions only) start in 1932 when the Labour Ministry began to collect information.[9] After the Second World War the number in unions rises until 1956 (apart from a drop in the politically troubled years of 1948–9), when they start to decline until the process is arrested in 1964. In the rural sector there is a great leap forward, from 1,706 in 1964, to 11,845 in mid 1967. But even in the non-rural sector there has been an increase of some 10 per cent during 1966 alone.

Union growth—and decline—seems to respond to several rhythms. Thus rapid economic growth and industrial development explains the rise during the war years. Since then the absolute increase of the labour force means that in terms of proportions of the total labour force the Chilean trade union movement is standing still rather than advancing. Internal political rivalries between Socialists and Communists held back growth in the late forties, as squabbling union leadership concentrated more on political than economic issues. Radical dominance in government explains the growth of 'unions' in the public sector, especially the white-collar public unions, Radicals being strong in the

[7] Details of early union movements are in Hernán Ramírez Nechochea, *Hisoria del Movimiento Obrero en Chile: Siglo Diez y Nueve* (Santiago, 1956); and Julio César Jobet, *Ensayo Crítico del Desarrollo Económico-Social de Chile* (Santiago, 1955). Both Ramírez (a Communist) and Jobet (an anti-Communist but left-wing Socialist) over-emphasize the organizational (though not the attitudinal) continuity in the Chilean labour movement.

[8] Hernán Ramírez Nechochea, *Origen y Formación del Partido Comunista de Chile* (Santiago, 1965), p. 93.

[9] These have been usefully summarized and analysed in James Morris and Roberto Oyaneder, *Afiliación y Finanzas Sindicales en Chile, 1932–1959*, INSORA (1961).

leadership. Administrative changes can influence the rate of union development. Simply by speeding up the process of legal registration the incumbent Christian Democratic administration has given a spurt to union numbers.

The present numbers in unions are shown in Table II below.

TABLE II

Unions: Structure as on 30 June 1967

Private Sector

Type of union	No. of unions	No. of members	% of unions	% of members
Industrial (or Plant)	1,076	175,332	34·8	53·5
Professional (or Craft)	1,666	132,679	53·7	40·5
Professional non-wage earning	136	8,283	4·5	2·5
Rural	217	11,485	7·0	3·5
	3,095	327,779	100	100

Source: Figures supplied by the Ministry of Labour. (But caution has to be used as there is a tendency in official government figures to include unions that have ceased functioning.)[10]

In comparative terms there are enough unionists in Chile (in relation to the total labour force) located at strategically important enough sectors of the economy (especially in the copper mines) for the union movement to have a powerful impact both in the economy and in politics. But before we can make any analysis, it is necessary to look at the way unions are organized, and in particular, the way in which the official labour code shapes the pattern of industrial relations.

Structure

The average Chilean union is small.[11] In 1960 roughly two-thirds of unions had under 100 members and only 5 per cent of unions have more than 500.[12]

[10] An INSORA study estimates that as many as 25 per cent of unions may not be functioning, with more or less 15 per cent of union membership in abeyance. Moreover, as some workers are members both of *sindicatos industriales* (hereafter plant unions) and of *sindicatos profesionales* (hereafter craft or white collar unions) there is an overlap of about one-sixth of total membership figures: ibid., pp. 26–7.

[11] The average union had a membership in 1965 of 141, which is very little of an improvement on 1930 when the average size was estimated at 130. Emilio Morgado, manuscript, INSORA. ngd.

[12] Barría, op. cit., from which much of the detail about collective bargaining has been taken.

The basic bargaining unit is the local plant union. Federations are difficult to form and, because of legal restrictions, may only carry out few and unimportant functions. Of the handful of major federations, two particularly strong ones, the copper workers and the maritime union, have special legal rights, and two others, the railway workers and the shoe and leather workers (*Cuero y Calzado*) work outside the restrictive legal framework—which is not the same as being illegal. None of the major central union confederations (most notably the *Central Unica de Trabajadores*, or CUT), are recognized in law, and their activities are more suitably dealt with in considering the political role of Chilean labour.

There are two major explanations of this localized, fragmented, and generally weak labour movement: firstly the code of labour law; secondly the economic structure of the country.

The legal code[13]

The legal code was laid down in the 1920s and has not been basically modified, apart from recent changes in the rural sector. Its intellectual origins lie in legislative projects devised by the two major political groupings of the time, the Conservative party and the Liberal Alliance. These projects were in essence authoritarian and restrictive. The major difference was that the Conservatives wished to see labour organizations controlled by employers (a form of Catholic paternalism), whereas the Liberals were prepared to see the government as the final authority. But neither inside the parties nor between them was there agreement on the need for legislation; most deputies were quite happy to see unions unrecognized and preferably nonexistent. It was only when Alessandri was forced by the military in 1924 to rush social legislation through that the code was accepted by the legislature. Organized labour, establishing a habit of Chilean political life, was consulted neither by the politicans nor the military: and it regarded the code as an attempt of the bourgeoisie to shackle it.

The labour code established two sorts of union:

(a) Industrial or plant unions could be established in enterprises with at least 25 workers, of whom at least 55 per cent must favour establishing a union. The decision once taken is binding on all members and there can only be one plant union. These may form

---

[13] James Morris in *Elites, Intellectuals and Consensus*, describes the historical background. R. Alexander, *Labor Relations in Argentina, Brazil and Chile* (New York, 1962), deals with the impact of the code on the industrial relations system. Interviews with union leaders in Chile, March to May 1966, added many details.

federations with other plant unions, but only for functions that have little to do with basic activities such as collective bargaining. The purpose of 'federation' is meant to be educational and social, though at the same time the code effectively prevents it from getting membership dues to finance even these mild forms of collective activity.

(b) Professional or craft unions which in theory are formed of similar trades or crafts across plant lines. They can include *obreros* (or blue-collar workers) and *empleados* (or white-collar workers) and even employers; and workers may be members both of plant and craft unions. In practice the incentive to form a craft union is less than a plant union. Craft unions do not have the right that plant unions enjoy of sharing in profits—thus financial limitations prevent the creation of strong legal craft union federations. Most craft unions, unlike plant unions, are white-collar organizations, or sometimes small groups of skilled workers still classified as obreros. Nor is membership compulsory as it is in a plant union. Given the generally weaker incentive of white-collar workers to form unions, especially in a country where by virtue of status they enjoy many privileges not available to obreros, the major role in union matters falls to plant unions.

In several ways the labour code regulates union affairs so that as economic organizations they are weak. Paradoxically this economic weakness strengthens political commitment as an influence in the union movement, for weak unions seek support amongst political allies. Nevertheless, restrictions are severe.

Firstly, except for unions specially privileged in law, or where employers reach *de facto* agreement with unionists, union officials are not supposed to receive extra pay for their union activities, but are expected to work full time at their non-union occupation. This hinders the development of a bureaucratic structure held to be typical of organizations with the social and economic characteristics of unions.[14] The effect of the present system, in the absence of substantial status, financial or power inducements for union office, is to increase political

---

[14] S. Lipset, 'The Political Process in Trade Unions: a Theoretical Statement', in W. Galenson and S. Lipset (eds.), *Labor and Trade Unionism* (New York, 1960). Nevertheless, there is a surprising amount of stability in office. A survey of the incumbents of the presidency (the most important post) of nearly all the industrial unions in the Santiago, Valparaíso, Concepción area found that 23 per cent had been president for 10 years or more, and 44 per cent for 5 years or more. Landsberger *et al.*, *El pensamiento del dirigente sindical chileno*, p. 22.

H

commitment as a motive for seeking office. Because union leaders are very often politically committed they seek office in the unions, and are encouraged by their party to do so; and divisions within unions run along party lines.

Secondly, unions may not keep funds aside for strike purposes. Though there is considerable evasion of this law, nevertheless, in financial matters the state closely regulates the unions. Union budgets must be submitted to local labour inspectors; union treasurers may keep only a derisory amount of cash in hand, and the rest in a supervised bank account. When unions need to act they must, because of the inadequacy of their own resources, either seek political help or mount only a 'guerrilla' strike—short, sometimes violent, often accompanied by seizure of the plant. They do not have the means to sustain prolonged action.

Linked to the problems created by state control is the general one of inadequacy of union funds. Much of the revenue of plant unions comes from profit-sharing schemes rather than from the members. In 1948 it was estimated that two-thirds of total revenue came from profits paid over by employers directly to the unions.[15] In 1959, the proportion of union revenue from profits was estimated at 52 per cent.[16] Yet there is still widespread evasion by employers; of the 608 plant unions entitled to receive profits in 1960 for example, only 265 received them.[17] Much union time is spent in squabbling with employers over profits. As the original Conservative scheme foresaw, the system of sharing profits increased employer domination and weakened worker solidarity. Craft unions and federations (apart from legally privileged ones) do not receive profits, and given the generally low revenue from dues, their financial weakness prohibits much activity. CUT, the major confederation, is in a state of continuous financial crisis.[18]

In general, union income from dues and profits is low, and limitations on power to invest prevent them from using their scarce resources to advantage; neither may plant unions pay any proportion of union

[15] Alexander, op. cit., p. 296. Employers also paid over a share of profits directly to their employees.

[16] Morris and Oyaneder, op. cit., p. 40.

[17] United States Department of Labor: Bureau of Labor Statistics, *Labor in Chile*, Report No. 224, May 1962. An estimated U.S. $777,000 was distributed; p. 37.

[18] Jorge Barría, *Trayectoria y Estructura del Movimiento Sindical Chileno*, INSORA (Santiago, 1963). Though it wishes to keep clear of international commitments, it was at one point forced to seek a loan from the WFTU; ibid., p. 313.

dues to the federation of which they may be a member. One study estimates that the average income per union member per month in industrial unions in 1959 was E°0·62; for professional unions it was E°0·29. Average income per member has been declining since 1940.[19]

Unions have little power or influence over the terms of employment of members. Contracting of labour is on an individual basis, in which unions play little part; and usually they have little power to prevent dismissal of employees.

The importance of the plant union, and the impotence of most federations, is heightened by the system of collective bargaining. Though one aspiration of the union movement is to move towards a system of national collective bargaining, and though there are eight federations that have achieved this, collective bargaining is essentially an affair of the local plant union. Bargaining over pay and conditions is carried out by local union officials for the individual plant, and does not necessarily set precedents for other enterprises. There is little need to form links with other plant unions if each one must engage in individual negotiations with employers. Moreover, the state closely regulates the methods of collective bargaining, and by its incomes policy attempts to limit the size of wage increases. Faced with this dual alliance of employer and state, unable usually to form alliances with other unions, the plant union is weak and in need of political allies; its problems transcend local conflict with their employer and become, because of state interference, issues of national economic policy.

One very important distinction established in the original labour code of 1924, and strengthened by statute and convention since, is that made between 'manual' and 'intellectual' labour, between obreros and empleados. White-collar workers, or empleados, are very favourably treated compared with blue-collar workers or obreros. In manufacturing industry, empleados salaries are three times as high as those of obreros. But apart from better salaries and automatic adjustments for cost-of-living increases, social services and benefits (an important part of salaries and pensions) also favour the empleado.[20]

[19] Morris and Oyaneder, op. cit., p. 42. In 1960 the Chilean Escudo (E°) was worth roughly one U.S. dollar.

[20] Though wage earners, in 1961, made up three-quarters of all insured persons, they received only one-third of benefits paid out; whereas empleados, one-quarter of the employed population received two-thirds of all benefits. Moreover, within the empleado sector, those in public employment received disproportionately more than those in the private sector—reflecting the Radical government's favourable treatment of one of its bases of support. United States Dept. of Labor, op. cit., p. 34. For discrimination against blue-collar workers in social security,

This division has important consequences for the union system. It tends to emphasize social distinctions within the labour force and so weakens it as a unified bargaining power; it encourages groups of workers classified as obreros to seek upgrading to empleado status. Since the state fixes the dividing line, its power to shift the line gives it a weapon against the labour force. Even though a craft union is less able to carry out typical union functions than the plant union, the individual benefits of white-collar status outweigh those of collective strength in a plant union of blue-collar workers.[21]

Collective bargaining, important in creating union solidarity, is practically the sole preserve of plant unions.[22] The major exception to this quiescence of empleado unions is amongst government employees, where according to a former government union leader and past president of CUT, unionization is in the region of 90 per cent.[23] The explanation for this is, in part, that because government 'gremios' or associations are not deemed by the state to be 'unions', many of the restrictive practices of the labour code do not apply to them. State employees are encouraged to form associations, and these take up union functions. Moreover, this rapid growth took place after the Second World War when the Radicals, losing their Socialist and Communist allies, were anxious to establish an alternative basis in the one sector of organized labour where they had influence—amongst their own employees. (Though the Radicals have lost influence in government unions of an 'industrial' kind, like railwaymen, they are still powerful amongst clerical and administrative occupations.) Government employees share a great advantage denied to most unions —one employer with whom to negotiate instead of a multitude. It is not surprising that unions, like the school-teachers or health-workers, should be amongst the most militant and successful in Chile.

---

see T. Davis, 'Dualism, Stagnation and Inequality: The Impact of Pension Legislation in the Chilean Labor Market', in *Industrial and Labor Relations Review*, Vol. XVLL, No. 3 (April 1964), pp. 380–98.

[21] Even unions under Communist control, such as those of Huachipato, Chile's steel plant, witness this tendency for small groups of skilled workers to form a separate craft union and seek upgrading of status. Interviews with Huachipato union officials, Concepción, April 1966.

[22] In 1965, of collective union demands, only 8 per cent came from empleado unions—which is hardly surprising as it was then illegal for empleados to make such demands as their salary increases were fixed by law. Barría, *El sistema de relaciones laborales.*

[23] Clotario Blest, 'Organización de la Clase Trabajadora', in *Punto Final*, No. 36 August 1967), p. 19.

The structure of the economy

Another important explanation of the fragmented union system is the fragmented economic structure. The large number of small unions mirrors the large number of small enterprises.[24]

Salaries and union strength vary closely in proportion to the size of the undertaking, because in the larger enterprises unions and management face each other in a collective bargaining situation like that of modern industry elsewhere.[25] In smaller factories employers tend to be paternalistic, if not autocratic, and some unions are undoubtedly company unions. The paternalistic environment of these factories and the docility of the work force is often explained in terms of the workers' social background. It is argued (and the observation has been made for most Latin American countries) that workers are recent rural migrants, whose value systems are conceived in the dependency terms of the rural *patrón*-peasant relationship.[26] This is now unlikely to be a major explanation, at least in Chile. One study shows that most migrants move not from the rural areas to the major towns, but through a variety of intermediate stages starting in small towns, before moving to the capital. Moreover, the survey found that recent migrants to Santiago had no special problems of adjustment to life in the city; their problems were those of the urban poor generally.[27]

Economic development in Chile has not, in the last decade, favoured the growth of an industrial proletariat, which would be the basis of a more powerful union movement. Manufacturing output between 1953 and 1965 grew faster than the number of workers employed, whose numbers increased only by 6·5 per cent, though the number of empleados went up nearly 40 per cent. In the mining industry, the

[24] In 1960, just under 50 per cent of the labour force in manufacturing industry was employed in units of five workers and less. Of the remaining half of the labour force in industry, 44 per cent work in large firms employing on average 500 workers; 40 per cent work in medium-size concerns employing on average 40 workers; and 16 per cent work in small firms employing on average 9 workers. There are only 26 large plant unions with over 1,000 members and only 5 professional unions of the same size. Barría, op. cit.

[25] Davis writes that, 'higher wage costs for larger firms result as a consequence of the fact that minimum wages and related protective labour legislation, as well as social security contributions (that may constitute as much as 50% of take-home pay) can only be enforced, together with tax and regulatory laws, upon the large scale, highly capitalized establishments'. Op. cit., p. 384.

[26] See E. Faletto, *Incorporación de los Sectores Obresos al Proceso* de Desarrollo, *ILPES*, Santiago (1965), mimeo. *Passim.*

[27] B. Herrick, *Urban Migration and Economic Development in Chile* (Cambridge, Mass., 1965), pp. 51 and 100.

work force fell by 12 per cent between 1957 and 1965.[28] The trend is similar in the modern steel plant of Huachipato.[29] This development, accompanied by the huge growth of the tertiary sector, obviously makes it difficult to apply European models of trade union development.

Unions in the economy

With inflation in Chile, unions have to run very fast simply to maintain the level of real wages. Workers' share in the gross national product since the Second World War shows that they have not been very successful, relative to other groups, especially as the taxation system was regressive until the Christian Democratic government. Average *per capita* income rose by 30 per cent between 1940 and 1954, but this was made up of a rise of only 9 per cent for *obreros*, compared with a rise of 38 per cent for empleados, and 43 per cent for employers.[30] Increases in output per man in mining and industry exceeded wage increases very considerably.

Strikes in Chile reflect concern with the cost of living; and the sort of strikes the unions mount are an index of their weakness. The number of strikes each year is closely related to the rise in the cost of living and the degree to which the government is committed to a severe incomes policy. A study of union activity between 1910 to 1926 also found that strikes varied with these factors.[31] Political affiliations may give strikes political overtones in Chile, but like union activity in most situations, the causes are basically economic.

Strikes are short, frequent, localized and mostly undertaken by plant unions on issues of wage demands and work conditions, rarely for wider issues such as union rights or a share in decision taking. There are far more illegal strikes than legal ones.[32] Illegal strikes are usually caused

[28] Central Unica de Trabajadores, *Política de Remuneraciones* (Santiago, 1966), p. 14.

[29] In 1953, a year after it was opened, it was producing 313,073 tons of steel ingots with a total labour force of 6,203 workers. But by 1964/5 it was producing 541,095 tons with a smaller work force of 5,510. Companía de Acero del Pacífico, *Memoria Anual*, 1965/6, Concepción, pp. 10 and 20.

[30] N. Kaldor, 'Problemas Económicos de Chile', in *El Trimestre Económico* (Mexico), Vol. XXVI, No. 2, April–June 1959, p. 179. See also O. Sunkel, 'La Inflación Chilena: un enfoque heterodoxo', in *El Trimestre Económico*, Vol. XXV, No. 4, Oct.–Dec. 1958; and A. Hirschman, *Journeys towards Progress* (N.Y., 1963), pp. 215–96.

[31] Jorge, Barría, 'Los Movimientos Sociales en Chile, 1910–1926', Thesis, University of Chile. 1960.

[32] In 1965 there were 274 strikes affecting 127,626 workers, and most of them were illegal. Alberto Armstrong Verdugo, 'Las Huelgas en Chile en 1962: su magnitud y causas', Licenciado Thesis, University of Chile, 1964, *passim*.

by spontaneous workers protest against unilateral action by the management.[33] Less organized than legal strikes, they last a shorter period; on average five days as compared with twenty-two days for legal strikes.[34] Strikes become legal only after a long process of arbitration. Many unions try to avoid these lengthy procedures, but run the risk of having their strikes declared illegal and so being ordered back to work. Strictly speaking it is illegal to strike to enforce agreements made with employers. That this should be the most common cause of strike action however, illustrates the weakness of the unions in face of hostile employers, and the lack of union confidence in the legal system of conciliation.

POLITICS AND THE UNIONS

Union activity in Chile could hardly fail to be political. The government so regulates unions that in any process of bargaining between union and employer, the state is present, both by legal obligation and by the needs of economic policy. Unions and government are brought together as a result of programmes to combat inflation by a policy of wage restraint. Unions in very few countries happily accept such restraint; in Chile, where they are not even consulted, union leaders cannot but feel that their basic function—that of safeguarding the interests of their members—brings them into conflict with the government.

The real question, however, is not whether the unions are political but whether they are politicized. How far are their actions or methods or their general ideas derived from an ideology, or bound to party rather than union considerations?

This sort of question is rather arbitrary unless it is placed in a more general political context. The question of whether unions are a force for revolution cannot be answered unless the other parts of the revolutionary movement and situation are considered. Many left-wing Chileans, like Lenin, have a careful appreciation of the limitations of trade union action, especially as the results of those occasions when the unions engaged in direct electoral and political alliances were not happy.[35] Unlike Lenin, however, their conception of the positive role

[33] Ibid., p. 27. Petras offers a similar conclusion for the rural areas. He writes that 'the leading factor contributing to the growth of militancy, union consciousness and social solidarity in the countryside has been the violation of agreements by the landowners', op. cit., p. 19.

[34] Armstrong, op. cit., p. 39.

[35] As when they joined the Popular Front Government in 1938 and suffered

of the party is less clear in theory and hardly operational in practice.[36] Interviews with Marxist union leaders made it clear that they stressed their role in forming a working-class consciousness, but did not see themselves, at least in their capacity as unionists, as leaders of the political revolution, whether peaceful or violent.

The answer to the question of whether parties control unions will differ for the distinct levels of union organization. It is obviously more the case that the national confederations are political organizations than small plant unions. This question can be examined at three levels—the national confederations, individual unions, and individual members.

a. The National Confederations

Several national confederations exist in Chile, and all are divided one from the other along party lines. The major confederation, the CUT, is controlled by members of FRAP (even if the claims of unity of that alliance are increasingly tenuous), though the Radical party and the Christian Democrats are unwilling to sever all ties with the CUT, if only because many of its constituent unions also contain Christian Democrats and Radicals on their executives. The Christian Democrats have a loose organization, the *Comando Nacional del Trabajo*, that grew out of a 'unionists for Frei' movement in the 1964 presidential election. There is a clerical group, *Acción Sindical Chilena*, which had scattered power in the countryside; its relations with the Christian Democrats are far from cordial. The Anarchists and other small ideological groups maintain skeletal and non-operative national organisations.

The CUT is by far the most important.[37] Of the fifty largest federations and single unions, about half are affiliated to the CUT, bringing with them 60 per cent of all unionists.[38] Empleado unions have a separate national organization, the *Confederación de Empleados Particulares*

---

from the subsequent break-up of that alliance, and the legacy of bitterness it entailed between Socialists and Communists.

[36] The Marxist theory of different role of union and party is stated by Perry Anderson in 'The Limits and Possibilities of Trade Union Action' (in R. Blackburn and A. Cockburn (eds.), *The Incompatibles: Trade Union Militancy and the Consensus* (London, 1967), pp. 264–80). He writes that 'trade unions thus everywhere produce working-class consciousness—that is awareness of the separate identity of the proletariat as a social force with its own corporate interests in society. This is not the same thing as socialist consciousness—the hegemonic vision and will to create a new social order, which only a revolutionary party can create' (p. 274).

[37] The development of the CUT is best described in Jorge Barría, *Trayectoria y Estructura del Movimiento Sindical Chileno*.

[38] United States Department of Labour, op. cit., p. 39.

(CEPCh), but this has close links with the CUT, and most of its important constituent members are also affiliated to the CUT. Many of the unions of public employees are also, perhaps a little oddly considering the political affiliations of Chilean governments, affiliated to CUT.

The overwhelmingly party political affiliation of the various union delegates to the national conferences of the CUT is shown in Tables III and IV on pages 120-121.

The gradual elimination of groups other than the Socialists and Communists from the CDN is clear, though it is illustrative of the conflict between Socialists and Communists that only in one conference did they present a joint list for election. At conferences of the CUT, dividing lines are not so much between different trade union delegations as between different party groups. Lists presented for election to the CDN are not alliances of one union with another, but of members of the same party affiliation from different unions. Moreover the ties that bind union leaders together inside the CDN are party political ties, and these are the ties that also cause them to divide.[39] Political groups of unionists meet their party advisers before and during the conferences to discuss tactics and the choice of candidates to be included in the list to be presented for election, though the extent and power of this advice naturally varies from party to party.

The CUT is more noted for making declarations of faith, than in putting its strength to the test. In practice it is torn between the all-or-nothing, anti-capitalist, class-war character of its statement of principles and the day to day needs of a fragmented union movement fighting not one battle but a large number of small skirmishes which are often more of a holding operation than an advance. The CUT has had little success in mobilizing workers for political action, except when the call to arms has coincided with the desire of some powerful single federation or group of unions to strike for economic ends. Political aims are tagged on to an essentially economic cause. Nor is it the practice of powerful unions to consult with the CUT before issuing a strike notice.[40] The

[39] The recent split in the Socialist Party, late 1967, produced splits inside the CDN of the CUT, as various union leaders aligned with one or other of the two Socialist Parties.

[40] Barría, op. cit., p. 264, quotes the report of the President of the CDN to the Second National Conference of the CUT, to the effect that few unions bother to consult with the CUT about their strike proposal, and that even worse, when they do do so, and the CDN opposes them, they still carry out the strike. 'In spite of the fact that there are very precise instructions in this matter, member unions ignore them. This has been the cause of the gravest internal difficulties inside the CUT'.

TABLE III

Voting for, and Composition of, Consejo Directivo Nacional of CUT

1953

List	Party	Votes	Councillors
List 1	Anarchist	188	3
List 2	Communist	903	13
	Socialist of Chile		
	Radical		
	Falangist		
List 3	Socialist-popular	657	9
	Socialist-dissident		
	Supporters of Ibanez—the ('Independents')		
List 4	Trotskyist	18	0
TOTAL		**1,766**	**25**
	Abstention	589	

Abstention (many delegations could not get to the conference, or could not stay—largely because of financial reasons. Later on political impediments also played a part.)

1957

List	Party	Votes	Councillors
List 1	Socialist and Communists	825	20
List 2	Radical Socialists-dissident	163	4
List 3	Trotskyist	18	0
TOTAL		**1,006**	**24**
	Abstention	354	

Abstention (mostly Christian Democrats and Anarchists. C.D. given 4 councillors to re-integrate them into CUT. Most anarchist groups had by 1957 withdrawn from CUT.)

1959

List	Party	Votes	Councillors
List 1	Trotskyist	17	0
List 2	Communist	645	12
List 3	Socialist	405	8
TOTAL		**1,067**	**20**
	Abstention	373	

Abstention (mostly Christian Democrats and Radicals and Anarchists.)

1962

List	Party	Votes Retired	Councillors
List 1	Revolutionary groups		
List 2	Independent	12	0
List 3	Communist	751	6
List 4	Socialists	686	5
List 5	Christian Democrats and Radicals	583	4
TOTAL		**2,065**	**15**
	Abstention	349	

1965

List	Party	Votes	Councillors
List 1	Communist	890	11
List 2	Trotskyist	20	0
List 3	Socialist	696	9
TOTAL		**1,670**	**20**
	Abstention	434	

Abstention (mostly Christian Democrats and Radicals.)

Source: 1953–62 figures from Jorge Barría, *Trayectoria y Estructura del movimiento sindical chileno*. This is in turn based upon newspaper accounts, conference reports, and some inspired arithmetic. 1965 figures compiled from newspaper reports and conference records. The number of councillors *directly* elected changed from conference to conference.

TABLE IV

Political Composition of Delegates to CUT Conferences

Political allegiance	1953 No. delegates	%	1957 No. delegates	%	1959 No. delegates	%	1962 No. delegates	%	1965 No. delegates	%
Communist	503	21.3	514	39.9	645	44.7	751	31.1	890	42.3
Socialist										
Popular	300	12.7	311	22.9	405	28.1	686	28.4	696	33.1
de Chile	100	4.2	—		—	—		—		
Disidente	200	8.4	41	3.0	—		—		—	
Radical	150	6.3	122	9.0	60	4.1	150	6.2	100	4.8
Christian										
Democ.	150	6.3	200	14.7	211	14.6	433	17.9	250	11.9
Anarchist	188	7.9	30	2.2	30	2.0	50	2.0		
Trotskyist	18	0.7	18	1.3	17	1.1	20	0.8	20	1.0
Independent	157	6.6	—		—		—		12	0.5
Non-classifiable and Absent	587	25.6	188	8.8	72	5.0	312	12.9	152	7.2
	2,355		1,354		1,440		2,414		2,104	

Source: ibid. Barría uses voting figures as an indication of political allegiance of delegates. By no means as accurate as the above table would seem to indicate, it is nonetheless, a broad guide.

impact of the CUT on union structure has been minimal. Two of its strongest desires are to create single union structures for each industry, and to present a single across the board wage claim for industries rather than the existing plant by plant system of negotiation, but little has been achieved.[41]

The CUT does to some extent advise unions, especially on strikes, and acts as an intermediary between government and unions, though in this role it is less important than the individual congressmen who carry out the same function, but who have the major advantage of regular access to the government system.

Generally the government ignores the CUT as much as possible.

[41] Barría, op. cit., p. 260, writes that 'in spite of the resolutions taken and the interest that has been aroused, little has been done in this field (i.e. the formation of single industry-wide unions) and the CDN as a body has taken no positive action, except for sending around circulars and propaganda. . . .' Moreover, he writes that nothing has been done about trying to spread union organization to the unorganized, partly because the CUT has not succeeded in organizing itself properly.

But even if this were not so, the grave financial weakness of the CUT would limit its action very severely.[42] An important role of the CUT is to provide a forum inside which the major ideological tendencies within the Chilean labour movement may debate policies and tactics. Its intransigence symbolizes the radical tradition of labour politics in Chile; its weakness mirrors the powerlessness of the labour movement as a *movement*, because, like the unions generally, the CUT is under-financed and under-manned, but also because, though it rejects the 'system' in the name of working-class unity, it cannot, in practice, fail to work within it in its daily struggle for members' conditions.[43] Indeed, organizational success, whether in creating effective industry-wide unions or in unionizing larger numbers of workers, might undermine the radicalism of the CUT precisely because that radicalism stems from a weakness which engenders a sense of frustration which seeks analysis and comfort in extreme solutions and positions.

b. The individual unions and federations

Most important unions elect their leadership on political grounds. Candidates for union office are usually known as members of or sympathizers with a party. Surveys carried out by INSORA, moreover, show that a near majority of union presidents in Santiago, Concepción, and Valparaíso are supporters of FRAP[44] (even if the survey also showed that political aims had to take second place to the daily routine of fighting for limited economic gains). The larger the union the more likely the politicization of its leadership.[45] But reliable data on the political affiliations of many union leaders does not exist, and especially

---

[42] Barría, op. cit., p. 295, writes that since 1956 the CUT has had to obtain over 70 per cent of its income by means other than the regular dues it is supposed to receive from its members.

[43] The radicalism of the Chilean labour movement is a mixture of two tendencies; on the one hand a radicalism that means essentially a rejection of the system, a spurning of involvement in the intrigues of a despised parliamentary system, a radicalism that places more value on purity of motive than effectiveness of deed; and on the other, a radicalism whose aim is of ultimate and complete transformation, but which is to be achieved by working within the parliamentary system. These two sorts of radicalism have, of course, divided the socialist world since the nineteenth century; and in Chile this division is still very marked.

[44] Henry Landsberger, et al., op. cit., p. 27.

[45] It is not difficult to find out, for example, that the leadership of the *Confederación de Trabajadores de Cobre* (CTC) is composed of seven Socialists, four Communists, one Independent and one Christian Democrat, or that the railway workers (FIFCh) has a leadership made up of four Socialists, three Radicals, three Christian Democrats and one Communist, and that the state white-collar

in the smaller factories there are many genuine independents, or leaders who are so popular that they can accept party affiliation on their own terms and dictate to the party rather than be dictated to.

Parties take an active interest in union elections, and the existence of party affiliation encourages a high turnout[46] in part because there is often an election campaign fought on party lines. There will usually be consultations with the appropriate party apparatus over the list of candidates, and the party will advise and assess candidates. But it must be borne in mind that neither union nor party apparatus, with a few exceptions, are well organized machines, and there is considerable amateurism about the whole process.

This amateurism must be stressed when considering the question of whether, as is frequently alleged, the parties, especially FRAP, *control* individual unions. One must also note that union leaders cannot normally mobilize members for other than limited, economic causes, because unions are legally financially and administratively weak. Nor do the parties always have a clear notion of what they want their union affiliates to do, apart from get and retain office. Another important factor impeding party control over unions is the fact that few unions are controlled by one party. Many union executives are composed of members of several parties, and this means that union policy must be the result of compromise. Even, or perhaps especially, Socialists and Communists are rivals for positions of power within unions and disagree over tactics.

Union leadership in Chile does not constitute a bureaucracy in the way that it does in Argentina.[47] Leadership in Chile is more vulnerable, more changeable, less powerful. On the other hand it is more political, in the party sense. Unionists stand for office because they are political; they rarely become political simply because they hold union office. There are not many reasons for wanting to hold union office in Chile, but political beliefs is one of them.

Another factor often under-emphasized, but which places severe limitations on supposed political control is simply that the major function of a union is to safeguard the living standards of its members. It may generate a working-class consciousness in so doing, but basically

---

employees, the *Agrupación Nacional de Empleados Fiscales* (ANEF) is led by seven Radicals, four Communists, three Socialists, and two PADENA (*Partido Democrático Nacional*). These figures refer to the position in June 1967.

[46] Interviews with union leaders produced estimates of between 60–90 per cent.

[47] Di Tella, *et al.*, op. cit., pp. 236 and 245.

its actions must revolve around pay and working conditions. Given the system of industrial relations in Chile, this is a full time, usually frustrating, procedure and can leave only little time and energy for more consciously educative and political activities.

c. The individual membership

The political role of the unions, or rather their politicizing role, can also be examined in relation to the political attitudes of members. Unionists are the group most likely to vote for FRAP candidates in national or municipal elections. This is especially marked in mining areas, but one study also shows that rural municipalities that border on mining municipalities are likely to have a higher proportion of FRAP voters than rural municipalities that have no common boundary.[48] The authors attribute this to the proselytizing role of the unions; though it is also possible that there is seasonal employment of rural workers in mines.

In general, left-wing voting is highest in areas where there are concentrations of unionists; male voters, who make up the bulk of unionists, are more likely to vote for Marxist parties than female voters; and surveys show voters who classify themselves as belonging to the working class are more likely to support Marxist parties than voters who assign themselves to higher social classes.[49]

One empirical study of the attitudes of union members shows that for coal miners in Lota, an isolated, depressed area, union membership was a very important agent of politicization; and this was still largely the case even for the more integrated workers in the steel unions of Huachipato who owed less to their unions in terms of impact on their attitudes and life style.[50]

There is considerable realm for speculation here on cause and effect; whether union membership is an active agent in promoting FRAP voting, or whether the political beliefs come before union activity. Nevertheless the solidarity of union membership with the Marxist parties does partly explain the emphasis that the Christian Democrats

[48] James Petras and Maurice Zeitlin, 'Miners and Agrarian Radicalism', *American Journal of Sociology*, Vol. 32, No. 4 (Aug. 1967). See also Glaucio Dillon Soares, 'Desenvolvimiento Económico e Radicalismo Político', *América Latina*, Vol. 5, No. 3 (July–Sept. 1962), pp. 65–83; and Glaucio Dillon Soares and Robert Hamblin, 'Socio-Economic Variables and Voting for the Radical Left: Chile 1952', *American Political Science Review* (Dec. 1967), pp. 1053–65.
[49] Guillermo Briones, 'La Estructura Social y la Participación Política', *Revista Interamericana de Ciencias Sociales*, Washington, Vol. 2, No. 3 (1963), pp. 376–404.
[50] Di Tella, *et al.*, op. cit., *passim*.

place on 'promoción popular'—the community organization of the so-called marginal groups outside the trade unions. Union membership in Chile does seem to have a socialization impact stronger than that e.g. of Brazil.[51]

RADICALISM, ISOLATIONISM, AND INDEPENDENCE

As a sub-system within the over-all political system, the union movement is characterized by radicalism, isolationism, and independence. It is remarkable that the movement has been able to maintain these characteristics, even though in relation to employers and the state it is weak, even though it must work within the system in its daily fight for members' standards, even though it suffers from internal ideological divisions, and even though it has abandoned its independence for a period of unsuccessful collaboration with other left political forces in the Popular Front era.

The Radical Tradition

Part of the explanation of these features must be sought in the roots of the movement. Sociologists of trade unionism stress the importance of the early character and structure of union leadership in forming a tenacious political tradition;[52] this would appear to be important in the radical tradition of Chilean unionism.

The early union movement in Chile was revolutionary and socialist.[53] Setting aside the parallel but weaker development of other unions like the Catholic unions, or the mutualist societies, the heart of early unionism was in the nitrate fields in the north. Recabarren, his own personality an important explanation of the radical tradition, was able to deflect a considerable tradition of spontaneous and disorganized popular protest into a revolutionary Federación Obrera. Founded in 1909 as a Catholic mutual benefit society, under Recabarren's leadership it discarded its origins, and in 1919 entered the Red International of Trade Unions as a candidate member. The isolation of the northern nitrate workers created the enclave condition favourable for the development

[51] In Brazil the dominant social framework would appear to be that of urban community rather than trade union. Azis de Simao, 'Industrialización y Sindicalismo en Brasil', in El Sindicalismo en América Latina (Barcelona, 1965), pp. 39–59. (Reprinted from Sociologie du Travail (Paris), No. 4, 1961.)

[52] W. MacCarthy, 'Why Workers join Unions', New Society, 26 Oct. 1967, p. 599.

[53] Jorge Barría, 'Los Movimientos Sociales en Chile, 1900–1910, Thesis, University of Chile.

of a radical union movement.[54] The appalling and oppressive conditions in the nitrate industry encouraged its extremism and rejection of collaboration with capital. Brutal suppression by governments made it hostile to the political system and legal authority. Intellectuals played little part in its ideological and political development, so that it was very much a *workers'* movement both in its political and economic activities. What it may have lost in political allies it made up in social homogeneity. The relatively lesser importance of immigrant workers from Europe made it a Chilean movement,[55] a national movement in a way unlike the labour movement in Argentina. Equally revolutionary, the labour movement was seen more as a movement of foreigners in Argentina. Finally the ideological commitment of Recabarren, coinciding historically with the impact of the Russian Revolution in Chile, was crucial in steering the union movement towards a Marxist position, even if anarchist strains were still strong.

This style of unionism was also gaining footholds in manufacturing areas of the centre of the country, though the anarchist tradition was already strong amongst port workers and some artisan occupations. The radical tradition was spread partly because of the unemployment of nitrate workers with the development of artificial substitutes following the First World War, and with the general depression of the inter-war period. Of 100,000 workers employed in nitrates in 1928, 60,000 had left by 1932. Migration patterns are not easy to establish, but there is evidence of the role of nitrate workers in spreading the northern style of unionism to other parts of the country.[56] The autobiography of Lafertte, a former secretary general of the Chilean Communist party supports this.[57] Even before he became a Communist of any note he had migrated to several parts of Chile, driven from the north by unemployment—and political persecution. He claims that his wandering existence was typical of the unemployed nitrate worker in this period.

[54] Kerr and Siegel note the importance of worker isolation as a factor creating a propensity to strike, op. cit., pp. 105–47.

[55] This point is made in a most interesting work by Adolfo Gurieri and Francisco Zapata, *Sectores Obreros y Desarrollo en Chile*, ILPES, Santiago (February 1967), mimeo., p. 9.

[56] Moisés Poblete Troncoso,'El Movimiento Sindical en Chile', *Combate* (Costa Rica), No. 23 (July–August 1962), p. 26, estimates that 20,000 workers (with families a total of 100,000 people) were moved from the north to the Santiago region by the government because of the unemployment following World War One.

[57] Elias Lafertte, *Vida de un Comunista* (Santiago, 1961).

Although the traditions of radical unionism were diffused generally by the nitrate workers, they were also taken up specifically by the copper unions, with the added factor of a sharper sense of nationalism, and its companion, anti-Americanism.

In many ways the copper workers, at least those in the large mines, are much better off than most workers in Chile and their unions are stronger. Their wages are three times higher than those in coal mining, and they enjoy a special legal statute allowing them to form a very powerful federation. But it cannot be argued that simply because the unions are more successful in their basic function of getting higher salaries that they are a labour aristocracy, becoming petit-bourgeois and separated from the rest of the labour movement. What is perhaps surprising, considering their privileged economic position, is their attachment to the radical tradition, whether it be measured by the political affiliations of their leaders, by the voting habits of their members, by their support for the CUT, by their militant strike record, or by their hostility to the agreements made by the Christian Democratic government with the American owned companies.

One interesting hypothesis explaining their solidarity has been advanced by Dillon Soares,[58] on the grounds that the occupational structure in mining and quarrying is far less favourable to individual economic betterment than in other sectors of the economy. In mining and quarrying, 83 per cent of the labour force is classified as obrero, compared with 56 per cent in manufacturing industry, 48 per cent in services, and 17 per cent in commerce. Though copper workers earn more than many empleados, this has been achieved through union solidarity rather than by upgrading of occupational status. The steel plant at Huachipato is less radical and less militant in part because more than half the labour force is classified as empleado. Moreover, the work force of Huachipato is less isolated and is much more integrated into its local environment than the copper workers.[59] This is not just a Chilean phenomenon; Kerr and Siegel have noted the greater radicalism of mining unions as compared with steel workers in several countries.[60]

There is naturally some degree of separation between union leaders

[58] Dillon Soares, op. cit., Table 2, p. 77.

[59] Di Tella, et al., op. cit., pp. 223-31 (Conclusion, by A. Touraine).

[60] Kerr and Siegel, op. cit., write that 'occupational stratification may be an unusually important aspect of industrial environment, affecting the location of the worker in industry and his propensity to strike. The iron and steel industry is often located in geographically isolated one-industry towns, and much of the work is arduous, yet it is not particularly famous as a centre of strike activity. It might rank somewhat higher were it not for the high degree of job differentiation

I

and militants, and those they lead. The politically active are in the minority—but they do shape the character of unionism. In copper-mining areas, there is still considerable support for non-FRAP parties, especially the Radicals who have traditionally been strong. And mining areas were likewise affected by huge increases in the Christian Democratic vote in 1964 and 1965. Yet the radicalism of the movement, even if it must be seen in its context of a mass membership that is far less active and militant than the leadership, remains an outstanding feature. It is important for the Chilean union movement that the best paid and best-organized sector of the working class should be seen to have achieved success precisely because of its militancy.

Unions and the political system: isolationism

For a state in which corporate interests have considerable representation in government institutions at all levels, the unions stand out by their absence.[61] The only institutionalized contact between unions and government is industrial conflict, where unions see the government as an ally of the employers rather than as impartial arbitrators. But of consultation or contact apart from that area, there is barely any.

Union relations with the government started badly when the original legal code was imposed on the unions. The code was paternalistic, and the unions were, justifiably, suspicious of attempts of the major parties to construct a framework to contain them (even though it is true that later the Communists saw advantages in legal protection, especially in the profit-sharing schemes). But unions' earlier hostility to what they had seen of the state—notably use of the army to put down strikes—was reinforced.

Since then, government and unions, as if by mutual hostility, have kept aloof. There is very little regular contact between them, and even that is seen in terms of dominator-dominated. It is true that the unions formed part of the Popular Front movement and government, but their role always was minor, and their representatives were seen as politicians in their own right and not as union spokesmen or representatives. The unions were brought into the major state planning agency created at this time, (the Chilean Development Corporation CORFO), but union members tended to speak only on matters concerning unions,

---

which marks the industry and which both separates the worker from one another and creates a ladder for each worker to climb' (p. 110).

[61] Constantine Menges, 'Public Policy and Organised Business in Chile: a preliminary analysis', *Journal of International Affairs* (Princeton), Vol. XX, No. 2 (1966), pp. 343–65.

were frequently ignored, and soon withdrew for good.[62] Today their corporate representation compares very unfavourably with that of business groups and farmers on state banks and planning agencies. In the crucial area of incomes policies, the unions have been ignored. And unions naturally mistrust a system in which there is considerable inflation and in which the share of national income of the obreros has been increasing less rapidly than that of other sectors. Unions have some representation on social security agencies, but the executive is very much in control and tends to designate and dismiss union representatives at its own will, so that in effect they are more account-able to the government than to their unions.

This isolationism is partly of the unions own choosing. Their interest in having representation is slight, because they also see the dangers of accepting responsibility for decisions in which they participate. In a different area, although Chilean employers are not noticeably keen about involving unions in managerial decisions, for their own part unions demonstrate an almost complete lack of interest in participation in management, let alone in a radical policy of workers control.

Unions and the political system: independence

To describe the unions as independent may seem odd when they are closely associated with Marxist parties. Yet for a number of reasons —partly because the parties are divided, partly because the tactic of the parties is to keep political and union activities in different compart-ments, at least in theory, and partly because of the memory of unhappy times when the identity of union and party became too close—it can be argued that the union movement wants to function independently. Individual unions and unionists are closely tied with certain political groups, but because they are not always the same political groups, there is a tacit agreement to recognize unions as separate agents with different functions.

But independence also means independence, unusual in Latin America, from the populist movements led first by Alessandri and later by Ibáñez, that drew along with them great mass, but not union, support.[63] Large numbers of unionists voted for these populist leaders,

[62] Manuel Barrera, 'Participation by Occupational Organisations in Economic and Social Planning in Chile', *International Labour Review* (Geneva), Vol. 96, No. 2 (August 1967), pp. 151–71.

[63] The movements supporting Alessandri and Ibáñez in the interwar period were mass movements, though of different sorts, in that Alessandri had mass support before he came to power, whereas Ibáñez was concerned to build up a mass base after he had taken power.

but the union movement as such never supported them, never ended up as the instrument of the state as happened under Vargas in Brazil, and to a lesser extent under Perón in Argentina.[64] Though Alessandri in his 1920 campaign attracted much popular support, and advocated measures attractive to the unions, union leadership was lukewarm. And that lukewarm attitude soon turned to hostility when Alessandri ordered the suppression of strikers in the nitrate mines at San Gregorio, and the destruction of the *Partido Socialista Obrera* headquarters in the province of Magallanes.

Ibáñez was similarly unsuccessful when he tried to capture the union movement by organizing a state-sponsored and supported union federation, the *Confederación Republicana de Acción Cívica* (CRAC). His movement attracted little support and was dissolved when he was overthrown in 1931. However, Ibáñez's codification of the labour laws passed under Alessandri, partly done to protect his own offspring, did increase legal unionism, when union leaders, mostly Communists, realized that there were advantages in legal recognition during a period of political upheaval and repression of left-wing movements.

Touraine explains union resistance to absorption in these populist movements largely because unions were weakly organized and had not developed a bureaucracy.[65] As there was no bureaucratic structure for the state to take over, the means of controlling the unions were not present. But if bureaucratic forms were weak, ideological commitment was not. If it is true that because there was no bureaucracy it was difficult for the state to take over the unions, the reason why the attempt failed must also be sought in the realm of doctrinal solidarity, reinforced by the homogeneity of the work force of the time, and its geographical and social isolation.

The concept of independence has a different meaning when applied to the relations between the unions and the Marxist parties. Historically when there was but one major party of the left, the Communist party, and one main union federation, the FOCh, the two were almost indistinguishable (though individual unions had less close links or, as in the case of the anarchist unions, were even hostile). But Communists now recognize that their failure to separate political and union activity was a tactical error that weakened the FOCh and led to its collapse.[66]

[64] Di Tella, *et al.*, op. cit., Conclusion, pp. 223–31.
[65] Ibid.
[66] Ramírez, *Origen y Formación del Partido Comunista*, writes that, 'The outstanding participation of communist militants in the FOCh. and the recognised leadership of Recabarren both in the party and in the union, the fact that FOCh.

There was little doubt of the closeness of the identity. The same people led both movements, Recabarren being especially prominent. The congresses of the party and the FOCh were held in the same place, one immediately after the other so that the same people could attend.[67] Policy pronouncements were issued jointly. When the Communists were persecuted by Ibáñez, it was inevitable that the FOCh should suffer and eventually collapse.

The great development of the Chilean left in the thirties was the formation of the Socialist party, born of the insurrection of 1932. With the Communist party, it propelled the labour movement to a new unity, forming the *Confederación de Trabajadores de Chile* (CTCh), in the union field, and the formation of the Popular Front in the political field. The existence of two powerful left-wing parties (and ideologies) competing for support in the unions meant that the fusion between party and union in the days of the FOCh could not be repeated. But the great error of this period was that both parties strove for hegemony in the unions. The CTCh joined with the Popular Front parties in the elections of 1938 and elected several candidates to Congress. But though the political role of the unions was relatively minor once the Radical-dominated Popular Front took office, the union movement suffered from the bitter divisions between Socialists and Communists that soon developed.

Socialists and Communists fought, sometimes even physically, for control. The CTCh broke up into two sectors, one Communist and one Socialist. But the split rendered the two confederations largely ineffective, especially when the Communist party was outlawed in 1948, and when many individual unions and federations, tired of the political in-fighting, withdrew from the CTCh.

The CUT was born in 1953, determined, from the stated intentions of its leaders, to avoid the fate of the earlier confederations. Both Socialists and Communists emphasized that union activities and party activities must be kept separate, and that union policy must be made

---

had expressed its sympathies for the Russian Revolution and had joined the Red International of Trade Unions, the circumstance that—from the very beginning—the party had intimate and harmonious links with the FOCh., were factors that created the impression that, for communists and enemies of the working class alike, the party and FOCh. were one and the same thing. . . .' 'This tended to divide the working class on the one hand, and on the other seemed to make FOCh., which was a mass organisation, the guiding force of the communist movement, which lessened its political weight. . . .' (pp. 209–20).

[67] Ibid., p. 210.

by unionists and not for them by the parties. Though unceasing in their attacks on successive governments, the leadership of the CUT has tried to avoid too close identification with the parties of the opposition —though not with real success.

CUT has by no means avoided the pitfalls of its forerunners. Socialists and Communists could present a united list of candidates to the congress of the CUT on only one occasion, and the growing tension of the various groups in the FRAP camp has transferred itself to the unions. Moreover both Christian Democrats, and, to a lesser extent the Radicals, have withdrawn from CUT, as have the extremist groups of anarchists and Trotskyists.

Conclusion

The line between political activity and union activity cannot be drawn with any accuracy for trade unions with such a marked ideological bias as in Chile. The logic of the ideological commitment that exists in Chile amongst union leaders is political commitment and participation in the fullest sense. Yet the interests of trade union unity and of effectiveness as economic agents of their members demands that union activity and party activity be kept as separate as possible.

Whenever the national confederations have become too closely identified with one party, or have become too closely involved in strife between the parties they have suffered. Union executives can contain members of several parties, but they can only live amicably together and function effectively as unionists if partisan differences are not transferred directly to the unions. Moreover, a strong part of the radical tradition of Chilean unionism is a mistrust of politicians as such. The legacy of anarchism in the union movement is a mistrust of parliamentary politics and the formal governmental system; and that mistrust has been reinforced by the frequent occasions on which members of the Socialist party, allegedly more revolutionary than the Communist, have accepted and remained in ministerial office under governments considered by unionists as their enemies.

This radicalism can be seen as the traditional behaviour of a weak and often dominated group that reacts against its condition of powerlessness by adopting a radical attitude of rejection. Because the union movement is weak, it cannot, at the national level, contain the party quarrels that break out amongst its militants. But because it also is radical, the attempt to start anew, to create a union movement free from political tutelage, is as common in its history as the break up of its fragile unity.

This radicalism does not have equal strength throughout the Chilean labour movement. The most radical and the most politicized are the national organizations, especially the national confederation. The least politicized and least radical (though they obviously have highly radical and politicized members) are the plant unions. But the plant unions are the unions with which most unionists have the major part of their contacts. Wages and conditions, the basic material of trade union activity, are the function of the plant unions. The radicalism of the CUT is thus not only a reaction against its weakness, but also a function of the fact that it does not, to anything like the same extent, engage in the central core of trade union activity. Yet the CUT and its activities, like those of its predecessors, cannot be dismissed or overlooked; its role may be seen as symbolic, but it is an important symbolism. Its radicalism, its isolation from the system, its attempts at independence from political tutelage, translate into political terms both the legacy of the traditions of Chilean unionism and the economic and social condition of most of its members.

THE PEASANTRY AND THE CUBAN REVOLUTION FROM THE SPRING OF 1959 TO THE END OF 1960*

by Juan Martínez-Alier

IN 1959 there were in Cuba about 500,000 agricultural labourers, 100,000 small tenants of various types, and 100,000 small peasant owners. I shall first give a short account of the conflicts that opposed landlords and small tenants. Then I shall proceed to study the more important conflicts between landowners (and farmers) and the labourers, and this will provide the occasion for some discussion of the writings of Draper and others. I shall also deal with the assumption often made that peasants want land while proletarianised labourers want higher wages and good employment. Finally, I shall explain the reasons behind the present drive for collectivization, which to some extent is helped and to some extent is hindered by decisions taken in 1959–60.

First, landlords and peasants, which in Cuba meant to a large degree American sugar companies and Cuban *colonos*—this was the term used for the sugar-cane growers. More than 90 per cent of all sugar cane was grown by colonos, the rest, known as 'administration cane', by the mills themselves. There were almost no plantations in Cuba, but many *colonias*, to use the Cuban term for farms of moderate size growing sugar cane and other produce and employing wage labour either exclusively or in addition to the labour supplied by the colono himself. Outside Cuba the impression has been given that the sugar-mill companies were themselves in charge of the agricultural operations. It was unfortunate that Ramiro Guerra's *Sugar and Society* was translated into English after the Cuban revolution without giving to the reader adequate warning as to how the situation had changed from

* This is a seminar paper given at the Latin American Centre, St. Antony's College, Oxford, in February 1969. Research was carried out in Cuba during 1968. The paper is based on an analysis of the correspondence between the Legal Department of the Agrarian Reform Institute and the Provincial Delegations and Zonas de Desarrollo Agrario, available at the National Archives, Havana.

the 1930s revolution on.[1] Guerra's book has been described as a 'good case study of the replacement of peasants by plantations'.[2] One must keep in mind, however, that this book, very influential in Cuban politics, deals with the situation in the early 1920s and even then it would have been an exaggeration, for the sparsely populated regions of Cuba, to say that plantations were displacing peasants. In some other regions, it is true that after the sugar market crashed following the 'dance of the millions' of 1920 and after the first restrictions on sugar output were introduced in 1926, some sugar-cane growers were replaced by 'administration cane' owned by the factories. They lost the land they had mortgaged.

In the 1930s the colonos mustered sufficient political force to create a powerful association and, riding the nationalist tide, they achieved favourable terms in their dealings with the sugar companies. Although they were unable to recover the ownership of the land they had lost, they achieved, among other concessions, complete security of tenure, regulated rents, and a fair share of the value of sugar. Not in vain had they found Guerra's book an 'admirable and patriotic' work which defended la clase más cubana, themselves,[3] and which drew attention to the political dangers of proletarization. Simultaneously, or not much later, all peasants—whether sugar-cane producers or not—got security of tenure and limitations on the level of rents.[4]

But the harm was already done. Desalojos (evictions) became a 'hot' issue in Cuban politics. Despite legislation, some peasants—though very few growing sugar cane—were now and then evicted in the 1940s and 1950s. Sometimes because they had installed themselves on private land alleging that it was public land. Sometimes because they had ceased to pay rents. Sometimes they left the land they occupied but received a substantial indemnity—this was known as vender la acción. And there were, of course, some genuine illegal evictions, much publicized, which had the function of keeping the question of desalojos on the boil. In the 1959 land reform law, only Rebel Army soldiers were given priority over desalojados (those who had been evicted) in

[1] The book first appeared as articles in Diario de la Marina in 1927. It was published in English (Yale U.P.) in 1964 with a preface by Sidney Mintz. Modern developments were mentioned but underemphasized.

[2] Eric Wolf, Peasants (Englewood Cliffs, N.J., 1966), p. 12.

[3] Asociación de Colonos de Cuba, Circulares Julio–Diciembre 1936, Anexo a Informe del Comité Ejecutivo, 12 Aug. 1936.

[4] This legislation is discussed in the Miami Cuban Economic Research Project publications, Cuba. Agriculture and Planning, pp. 207 ff., A Study on Cuba, pp. 343–4, and also in Batista's Respuesta and Piedras y Leyes.

getting land. From my study of the Agrarian Reform Institute papers it would appear that many desalojados received land who had not been victims of grave injustices. Some had got indemnities equal to their incomes in a whole year, a few seem to have been professional desalojados—persons who settled down into somebody's land and refused to move unless they were paid, repeating the operation time and time again; the alternative for the unfortunate landowners was a court case.

It is not difficult to understand why Cuban radicals—including *Bohemia*, the Communist party, and the Moncada programme—blew up the issue of evictions out of proportion during the 1940s and 1950s. They were giving notice to the American sugar companies that the settlement established in the Ley de Coordinación Azucarera of 1937 had come to stay, and would be made still more favourable to the colonos; never again would the Cuban nation allow plantations to displace colonos, and all land should be the property of Cubans. They were expressing their belief in the necessity of a numerous Cuban peasantry and therefore registering their protest when its ranks suffered a loss. The Communists, once they renounced or were made to renounce dreams of revolution after 1934, made of the defence of the peasantry and of anti-imperialism the cornerstone of their programme for alliance with the 'national bourgeoisie'. The radicals also felt it incumbent upon them to make a row every time an illegal desalojo took place because it had been Batista who had promoted, either while in office or as head of the army, much of the legislation protecting tenants; genuine desalojos, evictions of peasants without due process of law by the Guardia Rural ordered into action by *geófagos*, provided useful political capital. Such evictions proved that legislation meant little if the administration was corrupt: the creed of the *Ortodoxo* party.

It would seem, however, that the conflict between landlords and peasants over security of tenure had been reduced to manageable proportions before 1959. Landlords and peasants did continue to have conflicting interests on the level of rents, and here the legislation had not been enforced to the same extent, with the exception of the colonos. This conflict came into the open in 1959. The land reform law gave ownership rights to all kinds of tenants: cash tenants, share-croppers, etc. But the transfer of ownership rights was to be done by the Agrarian Reform Institute, after expropriation, and this procedure could take some months or even years. In the meantime it was not clear in the law whether the peasants had to go on paying rents and shares. The Agrarian Reform Institute had to decide what instructions to give to its local officers in this matter. There was some vacillation because peasants did not wish to pay, landlords still felt strong enough to become indignant, and the Agrarian Reform Institute was trying to comply with a law which was itself ambiguous. It is significant that instructions came from the Agrarian Reform Institute stating that payment of rents in sharecropping—and also in emphyteutic tenure—could now stop because these were 'semifeudal' forms of land tenure. Payment from cash tenants must continue to be paid. In practice, however, it would seem that tenants—at least, small tenants—ceased to pay rents.

More important than conflicts between landlords and peasants were conflicts between landowners, and large farmers, and the labourers. Their study offers the opportunity for some reflections on the interpretations of the first years of the Cuban revolution put forward by Draper and Andrés Suárez.

First, Andrés Suárez. This is from an abstract of his book:

Foreign policy determined Castro's conversion to Communism. The 'peasant origin' of the Cuban revolution is no less a myth than the assumption of an active part taken by the C.P. The picture arises of a movement shaped largely by the impact of one man, whose purpose—to extend the revolution to other Latin American countries—made him join the Communist camp.[5]

To repeat: foreign policy determined Castro's conversion to Communism. However, Suárez's discussion of the agrarian question is poor, and I would suggest that a proper analysis leads one to the conclusion that the peasants played some role in Castro's conversion to Communism—not so much before January 1959 as afterwards.

While dismissing the importance of the peasantry and excluding from it the agricultural labourers, Suárez comments:

It is difficult to see how a segment that did not amount to 6 per cent of the economically active population and plainly did not have the avid hunger for land that was later discovered by observers (when Guevara started the myth of the peasant revolution) could have made an important contribution to the revolutionary situation in January 1959. . . .[6]

But, later, he says:

It should be noted that in this underdeveloped country neither Guevara nor the Communists were demanding wage increases or making any other demand

---

[5] From the abstract of *Castroism and Communism* (M.I.T. Press, 1967) in the *International Review of Social History*, Vol. XIII, 1968, Part 2.

[6] *Castroism and Communism*, p. 34.

on behalf of the workers who, if one includes the agricultural sugar cane labourers, make up the great majority of the Cuban people.[7]

The peasantry, therefore, if one includes the agricultural labourers, was not after all such a small segment of the active population; perhaps some 35 per cent made up, as I have said, of approximately 100,000 small owners, 100,000 small tenants of various types, 500,000 agricultural labourers.

Two points may be made at this stage. First, as Suárez correctly says, neither the extreme leftist Guevara nor the P.S.P. put forward demands on behalf of the agricultural workers. The second point, which Suárez conveniently forgets, is that the agricultural workers themselves put forward demands from January 1959 on, mainly the demand for 'work or land', a demand which had revolutionary implications. It must be remembered that seasonal and even permanent unemployment was high in Cuba, the average rate between 10 and 15 per cent, the seasonal peak for agricultural workers reaching perhaps 50 per cent. In so far as the labourers demanded assured work, they were behaving as proletarians. When they demanded land, as an alternative to assured work, they were behaving as peasants. When they demanded that the state should take over the farms or estates in order that they should have work assured they were again behaving as proletarians. When they themselves occupied latifundia they were once again behaving as peasants in a jacquerie. There is evidence for all these types of conduct during the period from the spring of 1959 to the end of 1960.

Draper, discussing Huberman's and Sweezy's *Cuba, Anatomy of a Revolution*, says:

For Marx, the notion that the peasants would have been the driving force of a socialist revolution would have been simply unthinkable. . . . The alleged role of the working class [which Huberman and Sweezy later introduced] in this revolution is just as fanciful as that attributed to the peasantry.[8]

Draper derides Huberman and Sweezy, saying that they

discovered via a translator that Cuban peasants do not want their own land, they did not even understand the question of owning their own land 'until it had been repeatedly rephrased and explained'. . . . If so [Draper remarks] the Cuban peasants are truly unique. . . .[9]

Draper then discovered, apparently by introspection, that peasants

[7] Ibid., p. 42.
[8] T. Draper, *Castro's Revolution* (London, 1962), p. 45.
[9] Ibid., p. 34.

wanted only land, and on the other hand he thinks that this wish did
not make them into the driving force of the Cuban revolution. I
myself think that labourers wanted land or work; this was also true of
some sharecroppers. Neither land nor work was made automatically
available to labourers by the land reform law of May 1959, because it
was a very moderate law.

I shall not go into a full account of the contents and ambiguities of
the land reform law. Suffice it to say that it guaranteed neither assured
work nor land to the half million labourers; it would have meant, if
literally applied, little difference to most of them since it allowed
landowners and large tenants to keep at least a thousand acres. Except
in Camagüey, where there was much pasture land and little agriculture,
in the rest of the country and especially in the densely populated areas,
there were few landholders whose farms exceeded this generous limit—
which was a minimum and could still be exceeded if the Agrarian
Reform Institute thought fit, as it frequently did. In Camagüey,
Oriente, Pinar del Río, Isle of Pines, and some regions of Las Villas,
fifty caballerías, and not thirty, was the limit for pasture land, i.e. 1,600
acres. One must be careful and not mistake ownership and landholding
under a tenancy title. It is true that American and Cuban sugar companies owned enormous amounts of land; but this land was in the hands
of colonos, large, medium-sized, and small.

The crucial issue, therefore, was what was to become of this class
of colono farmers, especially the medium-sized and large ones. The
law said that those who farmed land belonging to sugar companies,
or to other landlords, would be entitled to buy up to thirty caballerías.
Subsequent legislation which never appeared would have determined
the procedure. It would seem that the revolutionaries, in May 1959,
were thinking that a land reform which got rid of the American companies' landed properties and gave ownership of the land to farmers
and small tenants was good enough. Thus, Marcelo Fernández, then
secretary of the 26th July Movement, referred to colonos who had
between five and thirty caballerías (170 and 1,000 acres) as campesinos,
peasants, just as he did to those who held under five caballerías.[10]

Why this lack of animosity against the large colonos? Because the
revolution, to start with, was merely a nationalistic, anti-imperialist
revolution, and the colonos, whose existence meant that at least the
agricultural if not the industrial side of the sugar industry was managed
wholly by Cuban citizens, had always been strong nationalists. It
seemed a fair and coherent step forward to complete the work of the

[10] Speech in July 1959, Primer Forum Nacional de Reforma Agraria, p. 560.

1930s revolution, as the Moncada programme had promised. The 1930s had given tenants complete security of tenure and limited rents. Now it was the moment to give to colonos a larger share of the sugar yield in the mill, and also title to the land they farmed if they had not already got it; these were demands the Association of Colonos had always put forward.

In the expropriated portions over the limit of thirty or fifty caballerías co-operatives were to be formed. The land was not to be distributed to agricultural labourers, Fidel Castro explained, so that the government would not be accused of creating *minifundia*. In any case, the amount of land available would have been small: probably less, had the law been applied literally, than the amount of land farmed by co-operative *ejidos* in Mexico—hardly a socialist triumph. The government thought rather in terms of making more agricultural land available to co-operatives through drainage of marshes and by ploughing up pasture land. That Fidel Castro was thinking along these lines is shown by the amount of time and effort he spent in the marsh land of the Ciénaga de Zapata during the first months of the revolution— not exactly the behaviour to be expected of him had he been interested in rousing the rural rabble of the sugar lands.[11]

There is, nevertheless, the theory that, while it admits the moderation of the land reform law, maintains that Castro thought from the beginning to go beyond its bounds. Moderation was, then, a deliberate deception. This has been argued by Rufo López-Fresquet, a liberal, who was at the time Finance Minister, and who resigned in March 1960. He says:

This law, if legally applied, would have affected only the owners of some latifundia. . . . But [it] was set aside to make way for the agrarian reform that was finally effected, the unwritten one that Castro always had in mind, the one that dispossessed the landlords and gave nothing to the peasants, the one that destroyed the institution of private property and made the State the sole owner of all property. . . .[12]

Perhaps Castro had been all along a secret collectivizer, and perhaps he was expecting that pressure from the labourers against his moderate land reform law would make the law unworkable. The fact remains that the law was a moderate one, and that the peasantry thought it was

[11] See a description of Fidel Castro's adventures in the Ciénaga de Zapata in A. Núñez Jiménez, *Hacia la reforma agraria* (Havana, 1960).

[12] R. López-Fresquet, *My fourteen months with Castro* (Cleveland and New York, 1966), p. 115.

so and brought pressure for a more radical land reform. It was, in fact, a middle-class land reform law. Thus Hugh Thomas's view that its lower-class origins gave the revolution a genuine radical programme, cannot explain the moderation of the first agrarian reform other than on the supposition that Fidel Castro had been engaged in dissimulation and expected the labourers to protest—as they did.[13]

If the land reform law, as it stood, had been strictly applied, not much land would have been available to the state for the settlement of labourers. There is evidence to show that the labourers did not wait to be offered a job in a co-operative created in far-away Camagüey; anyway, only a few could have got jobs there because of the investment in housing and ploughing up of pasture land which would have been required and because there were not so many estates, even in Camagüey, which exceeded by a large amount the limit fixed for this province. Labourers felt, once the *zafra* of 1959 was over and unemployment grew, that they had a right to get land *in nearby colono land*. Or, if not land, they felt they had a right to have work every day; this is especially important because it was an apparently reasonable demand which did not require revolutionary convictions.

Thus, the Agrarian Reform Institute began to get letters, many of them coming from local trade union leaders of sugar-cane farms, asking the state to take over their management—irrespective of whether such farms exceeded the thirty caballería limit. For instance, from a small settlement in Oriente comes a demand for 'urgent intervention of those sugar cane farms in order to make available sources

[13] Hugh Thomas's essay appeared in C. Véliz (ed.), *The Politics of Conformity in Latin America* (Oxford U.P., 1967). He argued that the Cuban middle class cannot complain of a 'revolution betrayed' because most of Fidel Castro's followers in the Moncada attack and in the Granma sea voyage were lower class in origin. But Hugh Thomas's views on the Cuban social structure are explicitly based on Lowry Nelson's authority and little else. Nelson invented the proposition (in his book *Rural Cuba*) that in Cuba there were two and only two social classes. But Nelson interviewed a sample of rural Cubans which excluded labourers almost totally, as has been noticed by Brian Pollit ('Estudios acerca del nivel de vida rural en la Cuba prerevolucionaria', *Teoría y Práctica*, Havana, Nov.–Dec. 1967). Nelson's views on social class are not to be taken seriously because his sample was not well selected and because his definitions are not clear. Very few indeed of Castro's early followers were agricultural labourers. In any case, the land reform law of May 1959 was not very radical; Thomas makes no attempt to explain why. One explanation would be that suggested in the text—which I myself do not believe in and which Hugh Thomas does not put forward openly. Another explanation, more to the point, is Draper's thesis of a middle-class revolution 'betrayed'—but 'betrayed' because of pressure from below, which Draper is not willing to consider.

of work which would alleviate the reigning poverty, because the firm does not have the cane fields weeded'.[14] There are quite a few such demands backed by complaints against colonos who did not weed the sugar cane to the necessary extent, in the unemployed labourers' eyes, and had never done so. Similarly, landowners had never cleared bush from pasture land to the necessary extent; *chapear los potreros* goes the Cuban expression. The generic distinctive expressions are *dar condición a los campos* in order to *abrir los trabajos*.

That landowners were having, during 1959 and 1960, a difficult time in trying to get credit was not taken into consideration by the labourers. The credit mechanism was disrupted by uncertainty, especially the uncertainty as to who was really a *malversador*, owning property subject to confiscation for misappropriated assets. Banks were careful in giving credit. Landowners and farmers, therefore, had no money to pay for agricultural operations which could be put off for a while. Moreover, labourers successfully claimed increases in wages or arrears in wages due, or thought to be due, to them.

The amount of work which can be used up in weeding in a climate such as Cuba's is, of course, very great. But similar complaints from agricultural workers seem to be common in other countries where wage-labour latifundismo exists; that is, a system of land tenure and use of labour in which moderately large farms are cultivated by labourers, using mules or oxen and simple manual tools, and where cash crops are grown. In fact, I think there is something here which is rapidly approaching the status of a law; employment is given by landowners and farmers according to considerations of marginal productivity; labour is paid wages (or piece-rates) which are above its 'equilibrium' price as they remain stable and must remain stable in the presence of unemployment or underemployment; therefore there is available labour which is not used despite the fact that it could make a modest contribution to output. In the labourers' eyes, this wasted labour is a scandal. In the eyes or landowners, it just does not pay to employ this labour—it is *incosteable*, as they repeatedly told the Agrarian Reform Institute. Accusations of absenteeism, of lack of entrepreneurial spirit, to landowners are beside the point, although very common. The conflict arises precisely because of landowners' and farmers' entrepreneurial employment policy.

Whatever the Cuban landowners' and farmers' motivation, the fact

---

[14] From correspondence with Provincial Delegation of Oriente, 8 September, 1959: 'intervención urgente de aquellas colonias para abrir fuentes de trabajo que alivien la miseria existence, pues la empresa no limpia las cañas'.

is that there was a reservoir of labour in Cuban agriculture which landowners and farmers did not tap; or could not tap, because it would not pay to do so, because they would have been 'exploited' in a Pigouvian sense.

The question then arises, why did landowners and farmers not let or sublet land to labourers in the past, turning labourers into tenants? The extra output coming from the extra employment would presumably partly accrue to the landowners turned landlords. And in Cuba, as in other countries, one finds yet another regularity; legislation providing very considerable security of tenure and limiting rents had been enacted in the '30s and '40s and '50s, and it had self-defeating effects. This legislation, which arose from the prominent position of the colonos in Cuban politics, explains, in the words of one observer, 'the latifundistas' reluctance to let land to cash tenants or to share-croppers because they fear not to be able to evict them when it becomes advantageous to do so'.[15]

Thus, the greater part of the Cuban peasantry, increasing in absolute numbers, remained proletarian. The reluctance of landowners and farmers to let or sublet land is also explained by the loss of face involved in granting land to labourers; the attack on latifundia is carried out usually in terms of the doctrine of the 'social function of property', a principle incorporated into the 1940 Cuban constitution and which provided the rationale behind the giving of ownership title to all Cuban tenants in 1959. This doctrine is directed against *rentier* owners who fulfil no social function and therefore it implies owner operation, whatever the economic penalty and whatever conflicts may then arise with the labourers over unemployment. If tenants can never be evicted, if rents and sharecropping arrangements are regulated by law, if landowners lose face by becoming landlords, then of course landowners and farmers will resign themselves to farm with hired labourers.

Some of the tasks that unemployed labourers feel ought to be performed may well prove 'incosteable', too expensive, for landowners and farmers; more so if trade unions are important, as in Cuba, because wages are then likely to be set institutionally at points above the level they would otherwise reach. For a liberal-left government, as the Cuban one was in 1959, the situation is most disconcerting. They could not agree to the wastage of labour. On the other hand, by themselves,

---

[15] Miguel A. Monzón, 'Nuestra defectuosa estructura agraria', *Cuba Económica y Financiera* (June 1958), p. 15: 'la resistencia de los latifundistas a ceder tierra en arrendamiento o a partido por el temor de no poder desalojar a éstos cuando fuera conveniente'.

they had not planned to take over the holdings of landowners and
farmers who were entrepreneurially minded; in fact, they had been led
to believe by the experts that poverty and unemployment came from
a lack of entrepreneurship and also from the alliance between the rural
bourgeoisie and the urban bourgeoisie who lived by importing food
and other goods from the United States. But the government was
subject to pressure from the unemployed labourers.

In 1959 and 1960, the labourers saw that a few of them, very few,
got jobs in co-operatives. They also saw that tenants of various types
ceased to pay rents in money or in kind and were being given the
ownership of the land they occupied. They saw that some labourers
who, in the past, had been evicted from plots of land, were now re-
installed in those plots. In 1959 and 1960, therefore, labourers were
seeing that practically everybody got land provided they were not true
full-blooded agricultural labourers. Hence, letters to Fidel Castro
stating

I would wish to know whether we who work for wages have any rights
[to land] because I believe that we who work for wages have had a harder
time than those who paid rents.[16]

or

The workers' delegate of the Aljovín farm . . . demands on the workers
behalf the 'intervention' of all 49 caballerías because they are manoeuvering
to give to them the 19 caballerías to which they are entitled in a stony part of
the farm, the worst part. . . .[17]

They could not believe that this was actually the result of the literal
application of a land reform law heralded as the solution for Cuban
agrarian problems. Landowners and farmers had the right to choose
where they wanted to keep their thirty caballerías and, of course, they
chose the central buildings and the better soils.

It is not surprising, therefore, if the government, facing this pressure
from the labourers, went somewhat beyond what the land reform law

[16] From correspondence with Zona de Desarrollo Agrario Havana—6, 28 June
1960: 'Deseo saber si nosotros los que trabajamos a sueldo tenemos derecho pues
yo creo que nosotros los que trabajamos a sueldo hemos sido más sacrificados que
aquellos que pagan renta'.
[17] From correspondence with Zona de Desarrollo Agrario Havana—7, 12 Feb.
1960: 'Delegado de los obreros de la finca Aljovín . . . pide a nombre de los obreros
intervención total de las 49 caballerías porque de las 19 que les tocan, les quieren
dar la parte de piedra y más mala de la finca, estimando que es una maniobra. . . .'

might have led one to expect. In this, they had the help of a useful institution: *intervención*, which did not originally mean expropriation or confiscation but merely the taking over by the state of a firm, very often because of a labour dispute, and only for a short time. Since the 1930s, there had been over a hundred intervenciones, the first, and most famous, being that of the American electricity company in 1933. There was nothing especially sinister in the demands to 'intervene' farms or other firms. In the summer of 1959, the Association of Colonos, a very moderate body, asked on the same day for the intervention of forty-three sugar mills—one-fourth of all sugar mills—on the grounds that they had delayed payments for the previous crop and also asked that small colonos be entitled to pay for the land, the ownership of which was now promised to them under the land reform law, just to show off their respect for the rights of private property.[18]

The government was, besides, determined to end what to them appeared as the monstrous irrationalities of the Cuban economy. Many prominent Cuban sugar-mill owners, such as Julio Lobo and Suero Falla, had argued for years that restrictions on the production of sugar had been a mistake. Cuba should have pushed up production regardless of any short-term effects on prices, to beat all competitors. Everybody believed that import substitution of edible oils, pulses, maize, rice, could be increased further than it had already been. The problem of what to do with the mass of unemployed had been discussed time and again; there was the school of those who thought that there was room and capital to give them work in industry and services—such as Pazos in the 26th July Movement's Economic Theses—and those who already said that only 'agrarization' could absorb the unemployed.[19] The government, it will be recalled, had at the beginning a bias towards industrialization; it apparently believed that industry could easily absorb unemployment.

When labourers started to claim work or land, and for the state to 'intervene' farms on the grounds that they had weeds or bushes, the government was probably surprised, or at least not necessarily pleased. I do not see any other way out for them—except some measure of repression—than the one they took. The government, or rather the regional departments of the Agrarian Reform Institute, began to use

[18] Information on 'interventions' before 1959 is given in *Cuba Económica y Financiera*, May 1953, March 1954, February 1957 (p. 17). The demands of the Association of Colonos in *Cuba Económica y Financiera*, August 1959.
[19] For this debate on development strategy prior to 1959, see for instance *Cuba Económica y Financiera*, November 1954, May 1955.

the device of intervention against farms not always included in the provisions of the law. After January 1960, when the Supreme Court made available a very ample interpretation of the law, they could say that the law was not being altogether disregarded. I doubt whether the government themselves were convinced by this casuistry.[20] It would seem that they lost almost all of their initial interest in having a *Rechtsstaat* and private enterprise. Because they had enacted a very moderate agrarian reform law, they had to give up these two liberal props if they wanted to keep the loyalty of the labourers.

Even then, changes came too slowly for the labourers' wishes. In the papers of the Agrarian Reform Institute there are at least forty instances of invasions of estates by groups of labourers acting on their own initiative. This despite the severity of Law No. 87 of February 1959, which declared that anyone doing his own land reform and taking land under his own steam would lose the right to get land or to work in a co-operative. Suárez's interpretation of this law seems unconvincing; he says that it could be enacted because there was no pressure on the land. I would say that it *had* to be enacted because there *was* some pressure. Suárez gives what he claims to be the single instance of public disorder in this connection, in San Luis, Oriente.[21] López-Fresquet tells how Fidel Castro was interrupted at a government meeting by Raúl Castro who brought in the news that bands of peasants were taking over land in Oriente, and how Fidel Castro was very annoyed by it; López-Fresquet concludes that his anger was genuine because he had already plotted to socialize all land.[22] Thus we have forty-two instances of illegal occupation of estates by groups of labourers;[23] not enough perhaps to talk about a revolutionary situation or about a peasant insurrection, but surely enough, in such a small

[20] Decisions of the Supreme Court, Nos. 7 and 21. Article 48 of the land reform law said that the objective of the land reform was to achieve economic growth, and said that the Agrarian Reform Institute should take the necessary measures to this end. It was argued that 'intervention' of farms in cases not contemplated in the law was therefore not illegal, as it was said to be done in order to increase agricultural output or to prevent it from decreasing.

[21] *Castroism and Communism*, pp. 34, 51.

[22] *My fourteen months with Castro*, pp. 162-3.

[23] Rather, forty-two references to illegal occupations, some of them mentioning a generalized situation in a whole province. Thus, a telegram was sent in July 1959 to the provincial delegate in Matanzas: 'Investigate occupations of land *por la libre*. Those guilty of infringement will lose the right to the minimum allocation of land. Broadcast this by radio in that province'. (From correspondence with Provincial Delegation of Matanzas, 16 July 1959.)

country, to conclude that the peasantry played some role in pushing the revolution to the left and thus 'betraying' the expectations of the rural middle class.

Apart from the invasions, there are many successful and *some unsuccessful* petitions for interventions coming from groups of labourers; there are also many letters from individual labourers to Fidel Castro asking for land—I have seen some five hundred which is a remarkable number of letters since most labourers could not write—and there were hundreds of extra legal interventions: the local delegates explained to the Havana authorities that they were compelled to intervene, regardless of what the land reform law said, because there were so many unemployed labourers around. There was no peasant revolution before January 1959; but there was a risk of one later on because the unemployed labourers felt deceived when the promises implicit, in their eyes, in the propaganda on land reform as a solution for all evils failed to materialize.

Let us now study some of these demands from labourers. I have said that labourers unemployed during part of the year wanted work or land: that is to say, when they demanded land it was in order to have assured work. Demands coming from groups of labourers or from trade union leaders on behalf of groups of labourers usually ask for the intervention of a farm on the grounds that there is work to be done but that the landowner or farmer is not having it done. This is, so to speak, a perfectly proletarian position; in fact, they were asking for what amounted to the socialization of the means of production, although they never phrased it in such a way. However, I found a demand from a local trade union leader who, in the most parochial spirit, asked for land in order to grow *frutos menores*—that is, subsistence crops, root crops, maize, beans.[24] Many demands come from individual labourers who ask for land in order to be able to feed their families, or in order to keep a cow, or in order to build a little house. Here geographical factors help to explain this way of thinking; the habitat is dispersed in rural Cuba and a good diet—a sort of Irish diet—can be obtained from milk and root crops—cassava, sweet potatoes, etc.—with very little work indeed. There are a few demands from labourers which fall into the ultimate disgrace of asking for 'land to cultivate because he does not want to form part of a co-operative',[25]

---

[24] From correspondence with Zona de Desarrollo Agrario Camagüey—19, Oct. 1959.
[25] Provincial Delegation of Oriente, 13 July 1960: 'tierras para cultivar ya que no quiere formar parte de una cooperativa'.

or, another 'demanding land for himself alone'.[26] This way of thinking, supposedly very typical of peasants, probably derived support at the time from the government's policy of giving ownership title to all small tenant farmers. On the other hand, however, many labourers wrote to the Agrarian Reform Institute explaining their situation: 'since the sugar crop ended he has worked only four days; he demands work on any farm or, if that is not available, land to cultivate',[27] or 'demanding land to cultivate or work in a co-operative'.[28]

Two propositions may, therefore, be accepted. First, that the idea of getting land was one of the Cuban agricultural labourers' ideas. Secondly, that some wanted land for its own sake, some wanted it to have assured work. There is not much point in trying to give percentages of how many people thought in these ways. What is important to notice is that for the labourers it was not a strange idea to appropriate land belonging to others, and that many said that assured work in a state-managed farm was as good for them as having land of their own. Therefore, when the question is asked, as it is many times asked, are agricultural workers interested in higher wages and assured work, or are they interested in land? the answer must be that they are interested in both, or in either.[29] They can go quite easily, it would seem, in one or in the other direction. To the extent that they are interested in land, it would be proper to classify agricultural workers as peasants. But in fact, the labourers' views could be fairly summed up, in Cuba in 1959 and 1960, as: I would like land, but on the other hand I would not mind getting assured work; or, I would like assured work, but on the other hand I would not mind a piece of land.

It must be emphasized that in 1959 and 1960 the slogan of the Cuban authorities was 'land to the tiller', not 'land or work'. It is true that land expropriated where no former small tenants were settled was not given to labourers but to co-operatives—in order, as we have seen, to

[26] Zona de Desarrollo Agrario Las Villas—14, 15 Sept. 1960: 'solicitando tierra para él solo'.

[27] Zona de Desarrollo Agrario Camagüey—18, 12 May 1960: 'desde la terminación de la zafra sólo ha trabajado cuatro días, pide ocupación en cualquier finca, o en su defecto tierra para trabajar'.

[28] Zona de Desarrollo Agrario Oriente—28, 30 Nov. 1960: 'solicitando tierra para cultivar o trabajo en una cooperativa'.

[29] One of the many writers on agrarian affairs who asks this question is Prof. Henry A. Landsberger in his curiously entitled essay 'Función que han desempeñado en el desarrollo las rebeliones y los movimientos campesinos: Método de análisis', Boletín (Instituto Internacional de Estudios Laborales, Geneva, Feb. 1968), p. 13.

avoid the charge of *minifundismo*. But even then, it seems that in many co-operatives labourers were given little plots of land. More important, the number of agricultural labourers who got the opportunity to work permanently in the public sector was small till 1961, and continued to be so until the second land reform law in October 1963. After Playa Girón, in the spring of 1961, when a great deal of counter-revolutionaries' land was confiscated, approximately two-thirds of the labourers were still employed, or hoping to be employed, by private landowners. In 1962, unemployment was still worrying the authorities very much.[30]

There is, then, some truth in the view put forward by Sidney Mintz: 'a rural proletariat . . . inevitably becomes culturally and behaviorally distinct from the peasantry. Its members neither have nor eventually want land. . . . They prefer . . . wage minimums (etc.)'.[31] However, against this view, there are the demands we have examined from labourers asking for land, or asking for land or work. Even as proletarians merely interested in doing away with unemployment, they were led to be interested in getting land or in a change in the ownership of land. Many Cuban labourers, as is suggested by Mintz, were thinking of getting rid of unemployment first; but in order to do so, they developed an interest in the land and views on who should own and manage it. It seems that they saw their own management of it or state management as valid alternatives.

Let us notice that these agricultural labourers, despite their peasant-like interest in the land, put forward deceptively moderate demands: land *or work*. First they moved against unemployment. Then, perhaps, they began to think of equality, of doing away with the difference between manual and intellectual workers, with class differences, etc. Thoughts of the millennium, sometimes assumed to be the characteristic initial view of such people, came some time later. In the beginning labourers were mainly interested in a moderate reform: getting rid of unemployment. This reform, if taken seriously, may lead far in a regime of wage-labour latifundia.

It may lead far—in the direction of collectivization, that is—even in countries where the proportion of labourers is lower than in Cuba,

[30] Figures on the number of labourers who had got permanent jobs in co-operatives or state farms in A. Bianchi's study of Cuban agriculture in Dudley Seers (ed.) *Cuba. The economic and social Revolution* (Chapel Hill, 1964), pp. 108, 125. For unemployment in 1962, speech of Ernesto Guevara to the dock workers, 6 Jan. 1962.
[31] Preface to Guerra's *Sugar and Society*.

and the proportion of peasants higher. This is because among those peasants there are usually a large number of sharecroppers. Cuban sharecroppers, who in 1959 and 1960 seemed quite pleased when the Agrarian Reform Institute gave them ownership of the land, had petitioned the authorities some years before presenting themselves more as labourers than as peasants. Thus, they had asked that the government should force landowners and farmers to pay the minimum wage to sharecroppers when the value of their share was less than the money they would have made working for the legal minimum wage over the same period.[32] This is a demand which I have found to have also been put forward by sharecroppers in Andalusia and in the Po Valley. Yet another regularity: it would be proper to classify some sharecroppers as agricultural labourers.

The first Cuban land reform was meant to stop the shame of desalojos once and for all: 'the land to the tiller'. It is not surprising, therefore, that many labourers asked the Agrarian Reform Institute that they too be granted land. This is clearly shown in the demands for land of some desalojados. Thus, the son of the famous Niceto Pérez, one of the four or five peasant martyrs who had died in the past defending his right to occupy a piece of land, wrote to the Agrarian Reform Institute explaining that he wanted some land because he needed a place to build a little house and because he was working in a quarry loading stones and he had work only three or four days a week.[33] It seems fair to assume that if the slogan at the moment had been 'work or land', many desalojados and some sharecroppers would have asked for work and not so much for land. Many labourers asked, and still more would have asked, for land or work. Those who did, thereby showed to the authorities that, first, they had to carry out a more thorough land reform than they had initially proposed, and second, that this land reform could easily result in a socialist pattern of land tenure.

It took some time to convince the authorities. The first agrarian reform went beyond the limits set in the law, but still left most land in private hands. The second agrarian reform, in 1963, still left over 40 per cent of agricultural land in private hands.[34] There is now a

---

[32] Acta, 21 August 1942, Asamblea Nacional de Representantes de la Asociación de Colonos de Cuba, pp. 50-1.

[33] From correspondence with Zona de Desarrollo Agrario Oriente—25, 18 July 1959.

[34] Forty-three per cent still in 1966, according to *Cuba Socialista*, August 1966, p. 128.

drive for complete collectivization·. Perhaps because nowadays in Cuba nobody is without a job while many people feel they could do with more food from a plot of land, land hunger has been increasing in the last years and social resistance to collectivization is perhaps higher now than some years before. In 1959, it seems, there was more hunger for work than hunger for land, or rather, labourers wanted a great deal of land reform as a guarantee for work. This paramount desire to have assured work could even have applied to the case of sharecroppers and the like, who were given land ownership instead. Social resistance to collectivization was less than it is sometimes assumed, and perhaps also less than the Cuban authorities assumed.

The Cuban land reforms, because they lead to the substitution of uneducated labourers for competent farmers and landowners as administrators of farms, have not been conducive to an increase in agricultural production, at least up to now; apart from the effect of the changes in economic policy—first diversification, then emphasis on sugar again. It is also likely that security of employment has acted as a disincentive to effective work; thus, one is not surprised to find Ursinio Rojas, an 'old' Communist member of the Central Committee and trade union leader, advocating in 1964 something like sharecropping for sugar-cane labourers, as a form of incentive: each brigade would earn in proportion to yields in the fields it tended.[35] That the economic performance of state farms is not very remarkable is not surprising. What is worth noticing is that such thorough changes were effected and are now being continued with the complete collectivization of agriculture (complete collectivization being a condition to achieve an equalitarian distribution of goods), and that the country has survived it and that the system still holds together.

Let us now rapidly review the reasons for collectivization, that is the conflicts between the peasantry and the state. I see three main areas of conflict. One is, of course, over the supply of food—peasants sell in the black market or have little incentive to produce because of scarcity of consumer goods. The second conflict is over use of land; thus there is now a policy forcing peasants with land around sugar mills to sow sugar-cane, keeping only a relatively small area to grow subsistence crops for themselves, and the intention of this policy is to economize in transport costs. It is also forbidden to sow sugar-cane together with beans, or rice, or whatever, in different rows. Thus, peasants lose all power of decision over their land because the state

[35] In a paper to *Primer Forum Azucarero Nacional. Sección: Organización del Trabajo*, 8 Sept. 1964. A similar proposal had been put forward by René Dumont.

decides what they should grow on the land, partially with considerations such as increasing exports, or soil conservation, or re-forestation, in mind. In practice, I fear, sometimes impressive plans to change land use in an area—as around Havana—are taken, consciously or unconsciously, not so much for economic or geographical reasons as an excuse to take the land, or the power of decision on crops, from the peasants.

The main conflict, as I see it, is that arising over the employment of labourers by the peasants. In 1966 they employed *permanently* 10 per cent of agricultural labourers.[36] There are no figures on how many they employed temporarily. It is no use maintaining that Socialism in Cuba will mean equality and non-utilization of material incentives when peasants are ready to give land to labourers, as sharecroppers or even free instead of money wages, when they pay them at piece-work for the sugar-cane and coffee harvests and for other tasks, and when they pay them in food. It is difficult to change these relations unless everybody becomes a state employee. This is what is being done now: pressure is brought on labourers not to work for peasants, who are provided with free voluntary or military labour by the state. Few of the peasants are *formally* expropriated. Thus, Fidel Castro's repeated promises to respect peasant agriculture for thirty, forty, or more years, are not yet explicitly repudiated.

From an economic point of view, there is surely a lot to be said for the view put forward by Professor Warriner:[37] 'no underdeveloped country which is concerned to increase food production— and which is not?—can afford to risk [collectivization].' But the poverty of a purely pro-peasant standpoint in order to explain what is going on and why, is obvious to Professor Warriner. So, she says: 'the main theme of the book [is] the desirability of raising the peasants' standard of living.' Therefore, 'the Russian solution'—collectivization—'cannot be assessed in relation to the main theme of the book', because collectivization did not arise from a desire to raise the peasants' standard of living. Other social and economic aspirations must be taken into account. In fact, taking other social aspirations into account provides Professor Warriner with her main argument against collectivization. For, she says, 'ownership can be a powerful incentive'—and indeed it can. But why take into account only some social aspirations and not other aspirations—such as the desire to have work assured, such as the

[36] *Cuba Socialista*, August 1966, p. 128.
[37] *Economics of Peasant Farming*, preface to the second edition (London, 1964), pp. XIII, XXXIII.

desire for equality? It is true, or at least it seems to me, that satisfying some of these aspirations was, and is, not at all incompatible, in Cuba, with a Communist revolution; it is also true that it was not economically sound to take them into account—at least in the short run. A partial viewpoint is not useful if one is interested not so much in preaching what should be done in order to increase the peasants' standard of living as to explain what went on and is going on and why. In order to do this, one must take into account all social aspirations—not only those which are conducive to economic development, social peace, and private enterprise.

Going back now to the situation in 1959 and 1960, we have seen that the labourers' aspirations to get land, or to get work in state land, are explained by the existence of unemployment. Landowners and farmers thought it uneconomic to use this 'wasted' labour. As time went by, one may assume that this moderate aspiration—land or work —which had however revolutionary implications, was supplemented by the aspiration towards equality which was born later or rather which later became acceptable. What people think depends, in the long run, on what they are allowed to say. Complaints about lack of employment opportunities, and talk on the prospects for some kind of land reform had been very common in Cuba—equality had been a more dangerous thought which not even the Communists had dared to entertain since 1934 or 1935.

The Cuban government could have distributed land to the labourers, or could, as it did within limits, give them work in state farms set up on expropriated land. It gave ownership of land to sharecroppers who were not very different from agricultural labourers and who nowadays are being collectivized, although they were promised that they could keep their land indefinitely. Even if the more conservative decision of giving land individually to labourers had been taken, this decision would equally have alienated the support of the liberals. Núñez Jiménez, the head of the Agrarian Reform Institute said, in the summer of 1959, that the land reform meant the introduction of capitalism in Cuban agriculture and the disappearance of feudalism.[38] Whatever he was trying to convey by this quaint use of words, it is clear that Socialism was far from his thoughts. But it was the land of the colonos which was in question. It is all very well to defend an anti-absentee, anti-imperialist, anti-feudal land reform; but when governments wish to put reform into effect they seem to find sometimes that they had

[38] In speech to Rotary Club, Havana, 18 June 1959, included in *Hacia la reforma Agraria*, 1960, p. 64.

exaggerated the evils of the situation; the land is actually managed by resident landowners or by large local farmers. And it is precisely these people whom the labourers see as enemies, because it is they who take the decisions as to employment.

ADDITIONAL NOTES

[1] Besides the works cited in footnote 4, see also J. O'Connor, *The Political Economy of Pre-Revolutionary Cuba* (Ph.D. Thesis, Columbia Univ., 1964), pp. 62–71, 85, and the studies mentioned therein; also, M. Sánchez Roca, *El derecho de permanencia* (Havana, 1944), which includes the text of the Ley de Coordinación Azucarera. As far as sugar mill land was concerned, this legislation effectively discouraged the growing of 'administration cane' by favouring colonos over administration lands in the allocation of quotas. Discouragement was needed because the colonos had simultaneously achieved a better deal in the payment for cane at the expense of the mills. But, by granting so much security of tenure and fixing such a low level of rents for both sugar cane and non sugar cane growing occupants, this legislation also slowed down the trend towards letting and subletting land to labourers.

[2] I am thankful to Brian Pollitt for pointing out that some labourers had been able to grow subsistence crops in small plots during the off-season. The Agrarian Reform Institute refused to give titles to such 'semi-proletarians' unless they had cultivated more than one-fourth of caballería, on the grounds that minifundismo was an evil. Pressure for land also came therefore from this sector of the peasantry. (Examples from correspondence with Zonas de Desarrollo Agrario Camagüey-18, 10 August 1960, Las Villas–16, 8 December 1960). A typical complaint from a colono farming seven caballerías follows. A labourer 'who sometimes is paid by results . . . and who has lived on the farm since 1952, always as a labourer, as I may prove from the social security receipts and pay-roll sheets which I am obliged to keep . . . to whom I gave a piece of land to cultivate subsistence crops for himself and his family, but with whom I have never had any sort of business relation apart from the relation between employer and employee . . . he is now trying to convince the authorities . . . that he has a right to the land since he works it. I will not deny that he works the land. As a worker, he has to work if he wants to earn his wages. But this does not give him any rights to land since he is not a renter, or subrenter, or colono, or subcolono, or sharecropper, nor even less a squatter'. (Zona de Desarrollo Agrario Matanzas-9, 16 June 1960). Neither was he a Rebel Army member, nor had he ever been evicted. Therefore, as for the majority of labourers, there was no land reform for him.

NOTES ON CONTRIBUTORS

OSCAR CORNBLIT Associate Researcher at the Centro de Investigaciones Sociales, Instituto Torcuato di Tella (Buenos Aires).

EZEQUIEL GALLO Research Fellow at St. Antony's College, Oxford. Member of the Research Staff of the Centro de Investigaciones Sociales, Instituto Torcuato di Tella (Buenos Aires).

PETER FLYNN Lecturer in Latin American Politics at the University of Liverpool.

ALAN ANGELL Senior Research Fellow at St. Antony's College, Oxford, and Research Specialist in Latin American Politics at the Royal Institute of International Affairs, London.

J. MARTÍNEZ-ALIER Research Fellow of St. Antony's College, Oxford. Author of *La estabilidad del latifundismo* (1968).